Psalms
for the Soul

**THE BOOK OF PSALMS
FOR DAILY REFLECTION**

Garden City, New York

This Ixia Press edition, first published in 2024, contains the unabridged text of The Book of Psalms from the King James Version of the Bible, originally published in 1611. The questions for contemplation following each psalm were written exclusively for this edition.

Illustrations by gettyimages.com.

Library of Congress Cataloging-in-Publication Data

Names: Ixia Press, editor.
Title: Psalms for the soul: the book of Psalms for daily reflection/Ixia Press.
Description: Garden City, New York: Ixia Press, 2024. | Summary: "This edition of the Psalms, reprinted complete and unabridged from the Old Testament of the King James Bible, is designed to be a daily devotional with contemplation questions included"—Provided by publisher.
Identifiers: LCCN 2023053999 | ISBN 9780486853277 (hardback) | ISBN 0486853276 (hardback)
Subjects: LCSH: Bible. Psalms—Devotional use. | Devotional calendars.
Classification: LCC BS1430.54.P279 2024 | DDC 242/.5—dc23/eng/20240424
LC record available at https://lccn.loc.gov/2023053999

Publisher: Betina Cochran
Senior Acquisitions Editor: Fiona Hallowell
Managing Editorial Supervisor: Susan Rattiner
Production Editor: Gregory Koutrouby
Cover Designer: Mark Voss
Creative Manager and Interior Designer: Marie Zaczkiewicz
Production: Pam Weston, Tammi McKenna, Ayse Yilmaz

IXIA PRESS
An imprint of Dover Publications

Manufactured in China
85327601   2024
www.doverpublications.com/ixiapress

Whether a private prayer, lamentation, song of praise, or expression of thanksgiving, the inspired words penned within the Book of Psalms continue to strengthen the faith of countless souls.

This edition, containing all 150 psalms reprinted complete and unabridged from the Old Testament of the King James Bible, offers more than just chapter and verse. Questions for contemplation have been added after each psalm, as well as space to record personal answers and thoughts.

May this book provide yet another source of comfort, reassurance, insight, and edification as you continue your spiritual journey.

Psalm 1

Blessed is the man that walketh not in the counsel of the ungodly, nor standeth in the way of sinners, nor sitteth in the seat of the scornful.

But his delight is in the law of the Lord; and in his law doth he meditate day and night.

And he shall be like a tree planted by the rivers of water, that bringeth forth his fruit in his season; his leaf also shall not wither; and whatsoever he doeth shall prosper.

The ungodly are not so: but are like the chaff which the wind driveth away.

Therefore the ungodly shall not stand in the judgment, nor sinners in the congregation of the righteous.

For the Lord knoweth the way of the righteous: but the way of the ungodly shall perish.

Are you one who follows the way of the righteous or one who follows the way of the ungodly? How does this manifest in your life?

Psalm 2

Why do the heathen rage, and the people imagine a vain thing?

The kings of the earth set themselves, and the rulers take
counsel together, against the Lord, and against his
Anointed, saying,

Let us break their bands asunder, and cast away their cords
from us.

He that sitteth in the heavens shall laugh: the Lord shall have
them in derision.

Then shall he speak unto them in his wrath, and vex them in his
sore displeasure.

Yet have I set my King upon my holy hill of Zion.

I will declare the decree: the Lord hath said unto me, Thou art
my Son; this day have I begotten thee.

Ask of me, and I shall give thee the heathen for thine
inheritance, and the uttermost parts of the earth for thy
possession.

Thou shalt break them with a rod of iron; thou shalt dash them
in pieces like a potter's vessel.

Be wise now therefore, O ye kings: be instructed, ye judges of
the earth.

Serve the Lord with fear, and rejoice with trembling.

Kiss the Son, lest he be angry, and ye perish from the way,
when his wrath is kindled but a little. Blessed are all they
that put their trust in him.

Think about putting your trust in God.
Is that difficult for you to do, and if so, why?

Psalm 3

Lord, how are they increased that trouble me! many are they that rise up against me.

Many there be which say of my soul, There is no help for him in God. Selah.

But thou, O Lord, art a shield for me; my glory, and the lifter up of mine head.

I cried unto the Lord with my voice, and he heard me out of his holy hill. Selah.

I laid me down and slept; I awaked; for the Lord sustained me.

I will not be afraid of ten thousands of people, that have set themselves against me round about.

Arise, O Lord; save me, O my God: for thou hast smitten all mine enemies upon the cheek bone; thou hast broken the teeth of the ungodly.

Salvation belongeth unto the Lord: thy blessing is upon thy people. Selah.

Think of a time when you cried out to God for protection. Did He hear you? How did you know?

Psalm 4

Hear me when I call, O God of my righteousness: thou hast
enlarged me when I was in distress; have mercy upon me,
and hear my prayer.

O ye sons of men, how long will ye turn my glory into shame?
how long will ye love vanity, and seek after leasing? Selah.

But know that the Lord hath set apart him that is godly for
himself: the Lord will hear when I call unto him.

Stand in awe, and sin not: commune with your own heart upon
your bed, and be still. Selah.

Offer the sacrifices of righteousness, and put your trust in the Lord.

There be many that say, Who will show us any good? Lord, lift
thou up the light of thy countenance upon us.

Thou hast put gladness in my heart, more than in the time that
their corn and their wine increased.

I will both lay me down in peace, and sleep: for thou, Lord,
only makest me dwell in safety.

*Have you ever felt a great divide from family and friends
because of your faith in God? How did you reconcile it?*

Psalm 5

Give ear to my words, O Lord; consider my meditation.

Hearken unto the voice of my cry, my King, and my God: for unto thee will I pray.

My voice shalt thou hear in the morning, O Lord; in the morning will I direct my prayer unto thee, and will look up.

For thou art not a God that hath pleasure in wickedness: neither shall evil dwell with thee.

The foolish shall not stand in thy sight: thou hatest all workers of iniquity.

Thou shalt destroy them that speak leasing: the Lord will abhor the bloody and deceitful man.

But as for me, I will come into thy house in the multitude of thy mercy: and in thy fear will I worship toward thy holy temple.

Lead me, O Lord, in thy righteousness because of mine enemies; make thy way straight before my face.

For there is no faithfulness in their mouth; their inward part is very wickedness; their throat is an open sepulchre; they flatter with their tongue.

Destroy thou them, O God; let them fall by their own counsels; cast them out in the multitude of their transgressions; for they have rebelled against thee.

But let all those that put their trust in thee rejoice: let them ever shout for joy, because thou defendest them: let them also that love thy name be joyful in thee.

For thou, Lord, wilt bless the righteous; with favor wilt thou compass him as with a shield.

How does this psalm make you feel, particularly knowing
that the writer asks God to destroy his enemies?

ʻPsalm 6

O Lord, rebuke me not in thine anger, neither chasten me in
    thy hot displeasure.
Have mercy upon me, O Lord; for I am weak: O Lord, heal me;
    for my bones are vexed.
My soul is also sore vexed: but thou, O Lord, how long?
Return, O Lord, deliver my soul: oh save me for thy mercies' sake.
For in death there is no remembrance of thee: in the grave who
    shall give thee thanks?
I am weary with my groaning; all the night make I my bed to
    swim; I water my couch with my tears.
Mine eye is consumed because of grief; it waxeth old because of
    all mine enemies.
Depart from me, all ye workers of iniquity; for the Lord hath
    heard the voice of my weeping.
The Lord hath heard my supplication; the Lord will receive my
    prayer.
Let all mine enemies be ashamed and sore vexed: let them
    return and be ashamed suddenly.

Imagine the state of the psalmist who penned this cry for mercy.
Can you relate to such intense feelings?

Psalm 7

O Lord my God, in thee do I put my trust: save me from all
    them that persecute me, and deliver me:
Lest he tear my soul like a lion, rending it in pieces, while there
    is none to deliver.
O Lord my God, if I have done this; if there be iniquity in my
    hands;
If I have rewarded evil unto him that was at peace with me;
    (yea, I have delivered him that without cause is mine
    enemy;)
Let the enemy persecute my soul, and take it; yea, let him tread
    down my life upon the earth, and lay mine honor in the
    dust. Selah.
Arise, O Lord; in thine anger, lift up thyself because of the rage
    of mine enemies: and awake for me to the judgment that
    thou hast commanded.
So shall the congregation of the people compass thee about: for
    their sakes therefore return thou on high.
The Lord shall judge the people: judge me, O Lord, according
    to my righteousness, and according to mine integrity that is
    in me.
Oh let the wickedness of the wicked come to an end; but
    establish the just: for the righteous God trieth the hearts
    and reins.
My defense is of God, which saveth the upright in heart.
God judgeth the righteous, and God is angry with the wicked
    every day.
If he turn not, he will whet his sword; he hath bent his bow, and
    made it ready.
He hath also prepared for him the instruments of death; he
    ordaineth his arrows against the persecutors.
Behold, he travaileth with iniquity, and hath conceived
    mischief, and brought forth falsehood.

He made a pit, and digged it, and is fallen into the ditch which
  he made.
His mischief shall return upon his own head, and his violent
  dealing shall come down upon his own pate.
I will praise the Lord according to his righteousness: and will
  sing praise to the name of the Lord most high.

---

*What injurious thing have you done to another
that gave you pause?*

Psalm 8

O Lord our Lord, how excellent is thy name in all the earth!
who hast set thy glory above the heavens.
Out of the mouth of babes and sucklings hast thou ordained
strength because of thine enemies, that thou mightest still
the enemy and the avenger.
When I consider thy heavens, the work of thy fingers, the moon
and the stars, which thou hast ordained;
What is man, that thou art mindful of him? and the son of man,
that thou visitest him?
For thou hast made him a little lower than the angels, and hast
crowned him with glory and honor.
Thou madest him to have dominion over the works of thy
hands; thou hast put all things under his feet:
All sheep and oxen, yea, and the beasts of the field;
The fowl of the air, and the fish of the sea, and whatsoever
passeth through the paths of the seas.
O Lord our Lord, how excellent is thy name in all the earth!

Go outside, and explore and reflect on the majesties of creation.
How do these reflections draw you closer to God?

Psalm 9

I will praise thee, O Lord, with my whole heart; I will show
forth all thy marvelous works.

I will be glad and rejoice in thee: I will sing praise to thy name,
O thou Most High.

When mine enemies are turned back, they shall fall and perish
at thy presence.

For thou hast maintained my right and my cause; thou satest in
the throne judging right.

Thou hast rebuked the heathen, thou hast destroyed the
wicked, thou hast put out their name forever and ever.

O thou enemy, destructions are come to a perpetual end: and
thou hast destroyed cities; their memorial is perished with
them.

But the Lord shall endure forever: he hath prepared his throne
for judgment.

And he shall judge the world in righteousness, he shall minister
judgment to the people in uprightness.

The Lord also will be a refuge for the oppressed, a refuge in
times of trouble.

And they that know thy name will put their trust in thee: for
thou, Lord, hast not forsaken them that seek thee.

Sing praises to the Lord, which dwelleth in Zion: declare
among the people his doings.

When he maketh inquisition for blood, he remembereth them:
he forgetteth not the cry of the humble.

Have mercy upon me, O Lord; consider my trouble which I
suffer of them that hate me, thou that liftest me up from the
gates of death:

That I may show forth all thy praise in the gates of the daughter
of Zion: I will rejoice in thy salvation.

The heathen are sunk down in the pit that they made: in the net
which they hid is their own foot taken.

The Lord is known by the judgment which he executeth: the wicked is snared in the work of his own hands. Higgaion. Selah.

The wicked shall be turned into hell, and all the nations that forget God.

For the needy shall not always be forgotten: the expectation of the poor shall not perish forever.

Arise, O Lord; let not man prevail: let the heathen be judged in thy sight.

Put them in fear, O Lord: that the nations may know themselves to be but men. Selah.

This psalm has a similar message to that of Dr. Martin Luther King Jr., "the arc of the moral universe is long, but it bends toward justice." Do you believe that?

Psalm 10

Why standest thou afar off, O Lord? why hidest thou thyself in
  times of trouble?

The wicked in his pride doth persecute the poor: let them be
  taken in the devices that they have imagined.

For the wicked boasteth of his heart's desire, and blesseth the
  covetous, whom the Lord abhorreth.

The wicked, through the pride of his countenance, will not seek
  after God: God is not in all his thoughts.

His ways are always grievous; thy judgments are far above out
  of his sight: as for all his enemies, he puffeth at them.

He hath said in his heart, I shall not be moved: for I shall never
  be in adversity.

His mouth is full of cursing and deceit and fraud: under his
  tongue is mischief and vanity.

He sitteth in the lurking places of the villages: in the secret
  places doth he murder the innocent: his eyes are privily set
  against the poor.

He lieth in wait secretly as a lion in his den: he lieth in wait to
  catch the poor: he doth catch the poor, when he draweth
  him into his net.

He croucheth, and humbleth himself, that the poor may fall by
  his strong ones.

He hath said in his heart, God hath forgotten: he hideth his
  face; he will never see it.

Arise, O Lord; O God, lift up thine hand: forget not the
  humble.

Wherefore doth the wicked condemn God? he hath said in his
  heart, Thou wilt not require it.

Thou hast seen it; for thou beholdest mischief and spite, to
  requite it with thy hand: the poor committeth himself unto
  thee; thou art the helper of the fatherless.

Break thou the arm of the wicked and the evil man: seek out his wickedness till thou find none.

The Lord is King forever and ever: the heathen are perished out of his land.

Lord, thou hast heard the desire of the humble: thou wilt prepare their heart, thou wilt cause thine ear to hear:

To judge the fatherless and the oppressed, that the man of the earth may no more oppress.

Whom do you think of as "the wicked" whose "ways are always grievous," whose "mouth is full of cursing and deceit and fraud"?

Psalm 11

In the Lord put I my trust: how say ye to my soul, Flee as a bird
  to your mountain?
For, lo, the wicked bend their bow, they make ready their arrow
  upon the string, that they may privily shoot at the upright
  in heart.
If the foundations be destroyed, what can the righteous do?
The Lord is in his holy temple, the Lord's throne is in heaven:
  his eyes behold, his eyelids try, the children of men.
The Lord trieth the righteous: but the wicked and him that
  loveth violence his soul hateth.
Upon the wicked he shall rain snares, fire and brimstone, and a
  horrible tempest: this shall be the portion of their cup.
For the righteous Lord loveth righteousness; his countenance
  doth behold the upright.

Can you believe that an all-loving God hates "the wicked and
him that loveth violence"?

Psalm 12

Help, Lord; for the godly man ceaseth; for the faithful fail from
among the children of men.

They speak vanity every one with his neighbor: with flattering
lips and with a double heart do they speak.

The Lord shall cut off all flattering lips, and the tongue that
speaketh proud things:

Who have said, With our tongue will we prevail; our lips are our
own: who is lord over us?

For the oppression of the poor, for the sighing of the needy,
now will I arise, saith the Lord; I will set him in safety from
him that puffeth at him.

The words of the Lord are pure words: as silver tried in a
furnace of earth, purified seven times.

Thou shalt keep them, O Lord, thou shalt preserve them from
this generation forever.

The wicked walk on every side, when the vilest men are exalted.

---

*Think of a time recently when you have flattered with your lips,
but your heart did not match what you spoke. How can you do
better if you are faced with a similar situation in the future?*

Psalm 13

How long wilt thou forget me, O Lord? forever? how long wilt
thou hide thy face from me?

How long shall I take counsel in my soul, having sorrow in my
heart daily? how long shall mine enemy be exalted over
me?

Consider and hear me, O Lord my God: lighten mine eyes, lest
I sleep the sleep of death;

Lest mine enemy say, I have prevailed against him; and those
that trouble me rejoice when I am moved.

But I have trusted in thy mercy; my heart shall rejoice in thy
salvation.

I will sing unto the Lord, because he hath dealt bountifully with
me.

Note the change of tone from the beginning of the psalm to the end.
Why do you think this is?

'Psalm 14

The fool hath said in his heart, There is no God. They are
    corrupt, they have done abominable works, there is none
    that doeth good.
The Lord looked down from heaven upon the children of men,
    to see if there were any that did understand, and seek God.
They are all gone aside, they are all together become filthy:
    there is none that doeth good, no, not one.
Have all the workers of iniquity no knowledge? who eat up my
    people as they eat bread, and call not upon the Lord.
There were they in great fear: for God is in the generation of
    the righteous.
Ye have shamed the counsel of the poor, because the Lord is his
    refuge.
Oh that the salvation of Israel were come out of Zion! when the
    Lord bringeth back the captivity of his people, Jacob shall
    rejoice, and Israel shall be glad.

Describe how you feel when you read this psalm.

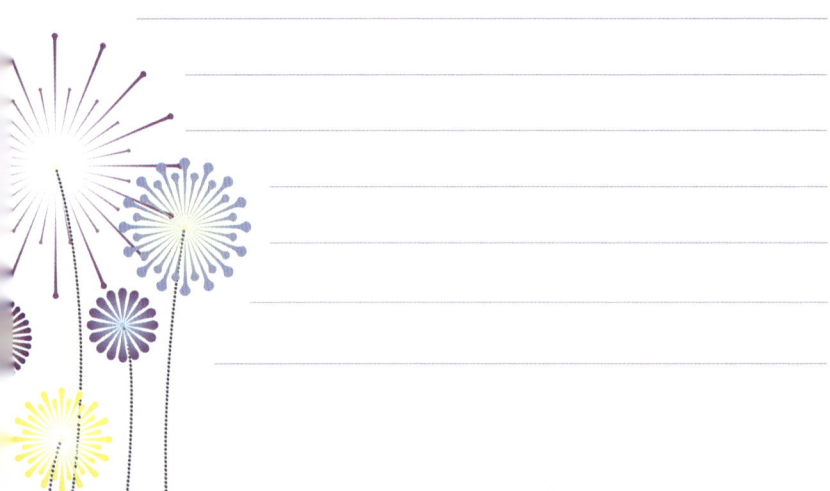

Psalm 15

Lord, who shall abide in thy tabernacle? who shall dwell in thy
    holy hill?
He that walketh uprightly, and worketh righteousness, and
    speaketh the truth in his heart.
He that backbiteth not with his tongue, nor doeth evil to
    his neighbor, nor taketh up a reproach against his
    neighbor.
In whose eyes a vile person is contemned; but he honoreth
    them that fear the Lord. He that sweareth to his own hurt,
    and changeth not.
He that putteth not out his money to usury, nor taketh reward
    against the innocent. He that doeth these things shall never
    be moved.

Who do you know that walks upright,
does what is righteous, and speaks truth?

Psalm 16

Preserve me, O God: for in thee do I put my trust.

O my soul, thou hast said unto the Lord, Thou art my Lord: my goodness extendeth not to thee;

But to the saints that are in the earth, and to the excellent, in whom is all my delight.

Their sorrows shall be multiplied that hasten after another god: their drink offerings of blood will I not offer, nor take up their names into my lips.

The Lord is the portion of mine inheritance and of my cup: thou maintainest my lot.

The lines are fallen unto me in pleasant places; yea, I have a goodly heritage.

I will bless the Lord, who hath given me counsel: my reins also instruct me in the night seasons.

I have set the Lord always before me: because he is at my right hand, I shall not be moved.

Therefore my heart is glad, and my glory rejoiceth: my flesh also shall rest in hope.

For thou wilt not leave my soul in hell; neither wilt thou suffer thine Holy One to see corruption.

Thou wilt show me the path of life: in thy presence is fulness of joy; at thy right hand there are pleasures forevermore.

What feelings do you take away after having read this psalm?

Psalm 17

Hear the right, O Lord, attend unto my cry; give ear unto my prayer, that goeth not out of feigned lips.

Let my sentence come forth from thy presence; let thine eyes behold the things that are equal.

Thou hast proved mine heart; thou hast visited me in the night; thou hast tried me, and shalt find nothing: I am purposed that my mouth shall not transgress.

Concerning the works of men, by the word of thy lips I have kept me from the paths of the destroyer.

Hold up my goings in thy paths, that my footsteps slip not.

I have called upon thee, for thou wilt hear me, O God: incline thine ear unto me, and hear my speech.

Show thy marvelous loving-kindness, O thou that savest by thy right hand them which put their trust in thee from those that rise up against them.

Keep me as the apple of the eye; hide me under the shadow of thy wings,

From the wicked that oppress me, from my deadly enemies, who compass me about.

They are inclosed in their own fat: with their mouth they speak proudly.

They have now compassed us in our steps: they have set their eyes bowing down to the earth;

Like as a lion that is greedy of his prey, and as it were a young lion lurking in secret places.

Arise, O Lord, disappoint him, cast him down: deliver my soul from the wicked, which is thy sword:

From men which are thy hand, O Lord, from men of the world, which have their portion in this life, and whose belly thou fillest with thy hid treasure: they are full of children, and leave the rest of their substance to their babes.

As for me, I will behold thy face in righteousness: I shall be
satisfied, when I awake, with thy likeness.

---

*"The apple of the eye"; "the shadow of thy wings"; "inclosed in their
own fat" . . . what phrase stands out to you? Why?*

Psalm 18

I will love thee, O Lord, my strength.

The Lord is my rock, and my fortress, and my deliverer; my
God, my strength, in whom I will trust; my buckler, and the
horn of my salvation, and my high tower.

I will call upon the Lord, who is worthy to be praised: so shall I
be saved from mine enemies.

The sorrows of death compassed me, and the floods of ungodly
men made me afraid.

The sorrows of hell compassed me about: the snares of death
prevented me.

In my distress I called upon the Lord, and cried unto my God:
he heard my voice out of his temple, and my cry came
before him, even into his ears.

Then the earth shook and trembled; the foundations also of the
hills moved and were shaken, because he was wroth.

There went up a smoke out of his nostrils, and fire out of his
mouth devoured: coals were kindled by it.

He bowed the heavens also, and came down: and darkness was
under his feet.

And he rode upon a cherub, and did fly: yea, he did fly upon the
wings of the wind.

He made darkness his secret place; his pavilion round about him
were dark waters and thick clouds of the skies.

At the brightness that was before him his thick clouds passed,
hail stones and coals of fire.

The Lord also thundered in the heavens, and the Highest gave
his voice; hail stones and coals of fire.

Yea, he sent out his arrows, and scattered them; and he shot out
lightnings, and discomfited them.

Then the channels of waters were seen, and the foundations of
the world were discovered at thy rebuke, O Lord, at the
blast of the breath of thy nostrils.

He sent from above, he took me, he drew me out of many waters.

He delivered me from my strong enemy, and from them which hated me: for they were too strong for me.

They prevented me in the day of my calamity: but the Lord was my stay.

He brought me forth also into a large place; he delivered me, because he delighted in me.

The Lord rewarded me according to my righteousness; according to the cleanness of my hands hath he recompensed me.

For I have kept the ways of the Lord, and have not wickedly departed from my God.

For all his judgments were before me, and I did not put away his statutes from me.

I was also upright before him, and I kept myself from mine iniquity.

Therefore hath the Lord recompensed me according to my righteousness, according to the cleanness of my hands in his eyesight.

With the merciful thou wilt show thyself merciful; with an upright man thou wilt show thyself upright;

With the pure thou wilt show thyself pure; and with the froward thou wilt show thyself froward.

For thou wilt save the afflicted people; but wilt bring down high looks.

For thou wilt light my candle: the Lord my God will enlighten my darkness.

For by thee I have run through a troop; and by my God have I leaped over a wall.

As for God, his way is perfect: the word of the Lord is tried: he is a buckler to all those that trust in him.

For who is God save the Lord? or who is a rock save our God?

It is God that girdeth me with strength, and maketh my way perfect.

He maketh my feet like hinds' feet, and setteth me upon my
high places.

He teacheth my hands to war, so that a bow of steel is broken
by mine arms.

Thou hast also given me the shield of thy salvation: and thy
right hand hath holden me up, and thy gentleness hath
made me great.

Thou hast enlarged my steps under me, that my feet did not
slip.

I have pursued mine enemies, and overtaken them: neither did I
turn again till they were consumed.

I have wounded them that they were not able to rise: they are
fallen under my feet.

For thou hast girded me with strength unto the battle: thou hast
subdued under me those that rose up against me.

Thou hast also given me the necks of mine enemies; that I
might destroy them that hate me.

They cried, but there was none to save them: even unto the
Lord, but he answered them not.

Then did I beat them small as the dust before the wind: I did
cast them out as the dirt in the streets.

Thou hast delivered me from the strivings of the people; and
thou hast made me the head of the heathen: a people whom
I have not known shall serve me.

As soon as they hear of me, they shall obey me: the strangers
shall submit themselves unto me.

The strangers shall fade away, and be afraid out of their close
places.

The Lord liveth; and blessed be my Rock; and let the God of
my salvation be exalted.

It is God that avengeth me, and subdueth the people under me.

He delivereth me from mine enemies: yea, thou liftest me up
above those that rise up against me: thou hast delivered me
from the violent man.

Therefore will I give thanks unto thee, O Lord, among the
heathen, and sing praises unto thy name.
Great deliverance giveth he to his king; and showeth mercy to
his anointed, to David, and to his seed forevermore.

---

*Do you consider God your rock and your fortress? In what ways
does He show up as these things in your life?*

_____

_____

_____

_____

_____

Psalm 19

The heavens declare the glory of God; and the firmament
  showeth his handiwork.

Day unto day uttereth speech, and night unto night showeth
  knowledge.

There is no speech nor language, where their voice is not heard.

Their line is gone out through all the earth, and their words to the
  end of the world. In them hath he set a tabernacle for the sun,

Which is as a bridegroom coming out of his chamber, and
  rejoiceth as a strong man to run a race.

His going forth is from the end of the heaven, and his circuit unto
  the ends of it: and there is nothing hid from the heat thereof.

The law of the Lord is perfect, converting the soul: the
  testimony of the Lord is sure, making wise the simple.

The statutes of the Lord are right, rejoicing the heart: the
  commandment of the Lord is pure, enlightening the eyes.

The fear of the Lord is clean, enduring forever: the judgments
  of the Lord are true and righteous altogether.

More to be desired are they than gold, yea, than much fine
  gold: sweeter also than honey and the honeycomb.

Moreover by them is thy servant warned: and in keeping of
  them there is great reward.

Who can understand his errors? cleanse thou me from secret faults.

Keep back thy servant also from presumptuous sins; let them
  not have dominion over me: then shall I be upright, and I
  shall be innocent from the great transgression.

Let the words of my mouth, and the meditation of my heart,
  be acceptable in thy sight, O Lord, my strength, and my
  redeemer.

How would you describe the glory of God?

_____

_____

_____

_____

_____

_____

_____

_____

_____

_____

'Psalm 20

The Lord hear thee in the day of trouble; the name of the God
of Jacob defend thee;
Send thee help from the sanctuary, and strengthen thee out of
Zion;
Remember all thy offerings, and accept thy burnt sacrifice;
Selah.
Grant thee according to thine own heart, and fulfil all thy
counsel.
We will rejoice in thy salvation, and in the name of our God we
will set up our banners: the Lord fulfil all thy petitions.
Now know I that the Lord saveth his anointed; he will hear him
from his holy heaven with the saving strength of his right
hand.
Some trust in chariots, and some in horses: but we will
remember the name of the Lord our God.
They are brought down and fallen: but we are risen, and stand
upright.
Save, Lord: let the king hear us when we call.

What does this psalm, recorded in Old English,
say to you in this contemporary era?

Psalm 21

The king shall joy in thy strength, O Lord; and in thy salvation
how greatly shall he rejoice!

Thou hast given him his heart's desire, and hast not withholden
the request of his lips. Selah.

For thou preventest him with the blessings of goodness: thou
settest a crown of pure gold on his head.

He asked life of thee, and thou gavest it him, even length of
days forever and ever.

His glory is great in thy salvation: honor and majesty hast thou
laid upon him.

For thou hast made him most blessed forever: thou hast made
him exceeding glad with thy countenance.

For the king trusteth in the Lord, and through the mercy of the
Most High he shall not be moved.

Thine hand shall find out all thine enemies: thy right hand shall
find out those that hate thee.

Thou shalt make them as a fiery oven in the time of thine anger:
the Lord shall swallow them up in his wrath, and the fire
shall devour them.

Their fruit shalt thou destroy from the earth, and their seed
from among the children of men.

For they intended evil against thee: they imagined a
mischievous device, which they are not able to perform.

Therefore shalt thou make them turn their back, when thou
shalt make ready thine arrows upon thy strings against the
face of them.

Be thou exalted, Lord, in thine own strength: so will we sing
and praise thy power.

Have you ever felt such abundance and blessings as the king mentioned in this psalm? How did it make you feel?

_____

_____

_____

_____

_____

_____

_____

_____

Psalm 22

My God, my God, why hast thou forsaken me? why art thou so
far from helping me, and from the words of my roaring?

O my God, I cry in the daytime, but thou hearest not; and in
the night season, and am not silent.

But thou art holy, O thou that inhabitest the praises of Israel.

Our fathers trusted in thee: they trusted, and thou didst deliver
them.

They cried unto thee, and were delivered: they trusted in thee,
and were not confounded.

But I am a worm, and no man; a reproach of men, and despised
of the people.

All they that see me laugh me to scorn: they shoot out the lip,
they shake the head, saying,

He trusted on the Lord that he would deliver him: let him
deliver him, seeing he delighted in him.

But thou art he that took me out of the womb: thou didst make
me hope when I was upon my mother's breasts.

I was cast upon thee from the womb: thou art my God from my
mother's belly.

Be not far from me; for trouble is near; for there is none to help.

Many bulls have compassed me: strong bulls of Bashan have
beset me round.

They gaped upon me with their mouths, as a ravening and a
roaring lion.

I am poured out like water, and all my bones are out of joint: my
heart is like wax; it is melted in the midst of my bowels.

My strength is dried up like a potsherd; and my tongue cleaveth
to my jaws; and thou hast brought me into the dust of death.

For dogs have compassed me: the assembly of the wicked have
inclosed me: they pierced my hands and my feet.

I may tell all my bones: they look and stare upon me.

They part my garments among them, and cast lots upon my
vesture.

But be not thou far from me, O Lord: O my strength, haste thee
to help me.

Deliver my soul from the sword; my darling from the power of
the dog.

Save me from the lion's mouth: for thou hast heard me from the
horns of the unicorns.

I will declare thy name unto my brethren: in the midst of the
congregation will I praise thee.

Ye that fear the Lord, praise him; all ye the seed of Jacob,
glorify him; and fear him, all ye the seed of Israel.

For he hath not despised nor abhorred the affliction of the
afflicted; neither hath he hid his face from him; but when
he cried unto him, he heard.

My praise shall be of thee in the great congregation: I will pay
my vows before them that fear him.

The meek shall eat and be satisfied: they shall praise the Lord
that seek him: your heart shall live forever.

All the ends of the world shall remember and turn unto the Lord:
and all the kindreds of the nations shall worship before thee.

For the kingdom is the Lord's: and he is the governor among the
nations.

All they that be fat upon earth shall eat and worship: all they
that go down to the dust shall bow before him: and none
can keep alive his own soul.

A seed shall serve him; it shall be accounted to the Lord for a
generation.

They shall come, and shall declare his righteousness unto a
people that shall be born, that he hath done this.

What parallels do you see between David and Jesus in this psalm?

_____

_____

_____

_____

_____

_____

_____

_____

_____

_____

_____

Psalm 23

The Lord is my shepherd; I shall not want.

He maketh me to lie down in green pastures: he leadeth me
   beside the still waters.

He restoreth my soul: he leadeth me in the paths of
   righteousness for his name's sake.

Yea, though I walk through the valley of the shadow of death, I
   will fear no evil: for thou art with me; thy rod and thy staff
   they comfort me.

Thou preparest a table before me in the presence of mine
   enemies: thou anointest my head with oil; my cup runneth
   over.

Surely goodness and mercy shall follow me all the days of my
   life: and I will dwell in the house of the Lord forever.

---

*Hold this most famous of psalms in your heart
throughout the day and experience its power.*

Psalm 24

The earth is the Lord's, and the fulness thereof; the world, and
   they that dwell therein.
For he hath founded it upon the seas, and established it upon
   the floods.
Who shall ascend into the hill of the Lord? or who shall stand
   in his holy place?
He that hath clean hands, and a pure heart; who hath not lifted
   up his soul unto vanity, nor sworn deceitfully.
He shall receive the blessing from the Lord, and righteousness
   from the God of his salvation.
This is the generation of them that seek him, that seek thy face,
   O Jacob. Selah.
Lift up your heads, O ye gates; and be ye lifted up, ye
   everlasting doors; and the King of glory shall come in.
Who is this King of glory? The Lord strong and mighty, the
   Lord mighty in battle.
Lift up your heads, O ye gates; even lift them up, ye everlasting
   doors; and the King of glory shall come in.
Who is this King of glory? The Lord of hosts, he is the King of
   glory. Selah.

What does it mean to you to have clean hands and a pure heart?
How is that made manifest in your everyday life?

Psalm 25

Unto thee, O Lord, do I lift up my soul.

O my God, I trust in thee: let me not be ashamed, let not mine enemies triumph over me.

Yea, let none that wait on thee be ashamed: let them be ashamed which transgress without cause.

Show me thy ways, O Lord; teach me thy paths.

Lead me in thy truth, and teach me: for thou art the God of my salvation; on thee do I wait all the day.

Remember, O Lord, thy tender mercies and thy loving-kindnesses; for they have been ever of old.

Remember not the sins of my youth, nor my transgressions: according to thy mercy remember thou me for thy goodness' sake, O Lord.

Good and upright is the Lord: therefore will he teach sinners in the way.

The meek will he guide in judgment: and the meek will he teach his way.

All the paths of the Lord are mercy and truth unto such as keep his covenant and his testimonies.

For thy name's sake, O Lord, pardon mine iniquity; for it is great.

What man is he that feareth the Lord? him shall he teach in the way that he shall choose.

His soul shall dwell at ease; and his seed shall inherit the earth.

The secret of the Lord is with them that fear him; and he will show them his covenant.

Mine eyes are ever toward the Lord; for he shall pluck my feet out of the net.

Turn thee unto me, and have mercy upon me; for I am desolate and afflicted.

The troubles of my heart are enlarged: O bring thou me out of my distresses.

Look upon mine affliction and my pain; and forgive all my sins.
Consider mine enemies; for they are many; and they hate me
with cruel hatred.
O keep my soul, and deliver me: let me not be ashamed; for I
put my trust in thee.
Let integrity and uprightness preserve me; for I wait on thee.
Redeem Israel, O God, out of all his troubles.

Familiarize yourself with the term "acrostic," of which this psalm is structured with the twenty-two letters of the Hebrew alphabet.

ʻPsalm 26

Judge me, O Lord; for I have walked in mine integrity: I have
  trusted also in the Lord; therefore I shall not slide.
Examine me, O Lord, and prove me; try my reins and my heart.
For thy loving-kindness is before mine eyes: and I have walked
  in thy truth.
I have not sat with vain persons, neither will I go in with
  dissemblers.
I have hated the congregation of evildoers; and will not sit with
  the wicked.
I will wash mine hands in innocency: so will I compass thine
  altar, O Lord:
That I may publish with the voice of thanksgiving, and tell of
  all thy wondrous works.
Lord, I have loved the habitation of thy house, and the place
  where thine honor dwelleth.
Gather not my soul with sinners, nor my life with bloody men:
In whose hands is mischief, and their right hand is full of bribes.
But as for me, I will walk in mine integrity: redeem me, and be
  merciful unto me.
My foot standeth in an even place: in the congregations will I
  bless the Lord.

What does it mean to you to "walk in mine integrity"?

Psalm 27

The Lord is my light and my salvation: whom shall I fear? the
    Lord is the strength of my life; of whom shall I be afraid?

When the wicked, even mine enemies and my foes, came upon
    me to eat up my flesh, they stumbled and fell.

Though a host should encamp against me, my heart shall not
    fear: though war should rise against me, in this will I be
    confident.

One thing have I desired of the Lord, that will I seek after; that
    I may dwell in the house of the Lord all the days of my
    life, to behold the beauty of the Lord, and to inquire in his
    temple.

For in the time of trouble he shall hide me in his pavilion: in the
    secret of his tabernacle shall he hide me; he shall set me up
    upon a rock.

And now shall mine head be lifted up above mine enemies
    round about me: therefore will I offer in his tabernacle
    sacrifices of joy; I will sing, yea, I will sing praises unto the
    Lord.

Hear, O Lord, when I cry with my voice: have mercy also upon
    me, and answer me.

When thou saidst, Seek ye my face; my heart said unto thee,
    Thy face, Lord, will I seek.

Hide not thy face far from me; put not thy servant away in
    anger: thou hast been my help; leave me not, neither
    forsake me, O God of my salvation.

When my father and my mother forsake me, then the Lord will
    take me up.

Teach me thy way, O Lord, and lead me in a plain path, because
    of mine enemies.

Deliver me not over unto the will of mine enemies: for false
    witnesses are risen up against me, and such as breathe out
    cruelty.

I had fainted, unless I had believed to see the goodness of the
   Lord in the land of the living.
Wait on the Lord: be of good courage, and he shall strengthen
   thine heart: wait, I say, on the Lord.

---

*Find and listen to the various renditions of "The Lord Is My Light
and My Salvation." What feelings does this song evoke?*

ʻPsalm 28

Unto thee will I cry, O Lord my rock; be not silent to me: lest,
if thou be silent to me, I become like them that go down
into the pit.

Hear the voice of my supplications, when I cry unto thee, when
I lift up my hands toward thy holy oracle.

Draw me not away with the wicked, and with the workers of
iniquity, which speak peace to their neighbors, but mischief
is in their hearts.

Give them according to their deeds, and according to the
wickedness of their endeavors: give them after the work of
their hands; render to them their desert.

Because they regard not the works of the Lord, nor the operation
of his hands, he shall destroy them, and not build them up.

Blessed be the Lord, because he hath heard the voice of my
supplications.

The Lord is my strength and my shield; my heart trusted in him,
and I am helped: therefore my heart greatly rejoiceth; and
with my song will I praise him.

The Lord is their strength, and he is the saving strength of his
anointed.

Save thy people, and bless thine inheritance: feed them also,
and lift them up forever.

Think about a time when you cried for mercy.
Did the Lord respond? Was it in the way you expected?

Psalm 29

Give unto the Lord, O ye mighty, give unto the Lord glory and
strength.

Give unto the Lord the glory due unto his name; worship the
Lord in the beauty of holiness.

The voice of the Lord is upon the waters: the God of glory
thundereth: the Lord is upon many waters.

The voice of the Lord is powerful; the voice of the Lord is full
of majesty.

The voice of the Lord breaketh the cedars; yea, the Lord
breaketh the cedars of Lebanon.

He maketh them also to skip like a calf; Lebanon and Sirion like
a young unicorn.

The voice of the Lord divideth the flames of fire.

The voice of the Lord shaketh the wilderness; the Lord shaketh
the wilderness of Kadesh.

The voice of the Lord maketh the hinds to calve, and
discovereth the forests: and in his temple doth every one
speak of his glory.

The Lord sitteth upon the flood; yea, the Lord sitteth King
forever.

The Lord will give strength unto his people; the Lord will bless
his people with peace.

Forces of nature are prevalent in this psalm.
What sensations do you feel?

_____

_____

_____

Psalm 30

I will extol thee, O Lord; for thou hast lifted me up, and hast
    not made my foes to rejoice over me.
O Lord my God, I cried unto thee, and thou hast healed me.
O Lord, thou hast brought up my soul from the grave: thou hast
    kept me alive, that I should not go down to the pit.
Sing unto the Lord, O ye saints of his, and give thanks at the
    remembrance of his holiness.
For his anger endureth but a moment; in his favor is life:
    weeping may endure for a night, but joy cometh in the
    morning.
And in my prosperity I said, I shall never be moved.
Lord, by thy favor thou hast made my mountain to stand
    strong: thou didst hide thy face, and I was troubled.
I cried to thee, O Lord; and unto the Lord I made supplication.
What profit is there in my blood when I go down to the pit?
    Shall the dust praise thee? shall it declare thy truth?
Hear, O Lord, and have mercy upon me: Lord, be thou my
    helper.
Thou hast turned for me my mourning into dancing: thou hast
    put off my sackcloth, and girded me with gladness;
To the end that my glory may sing praise to thee, and not be
    silent. O Lord my God, I will give thanks unto thee forever.

Do you ever thank God out loud for the blessings in your life?
Consider writing a thank-you note to God.

Psalm 31

In thee, O Lord, do I put my trust; let me never be ashamed:
deliver me in thy righteousness.

Bow down thine ear to me; deliver me speedily: be thou my
strong rock, for a house of defense to save me.

For thou art my rock and my fortress; therefore for thy name's
sake lead me, and guide me.

Pull me out of the net that they have laid privily for me: for
thou art my strength.

Into thine hand I commit my spirit: thou hast redeemed me,
O Lord God of truth.

I have hated them that regard lying vanities: but I trust in the Lord.

I will be glad and rejoice in thy mercy: for thou hast considered
my trouble; thou hast known my soul in adversities;

And hast not shut me up into the hand of the enemy: thou hast
set my feet in a large room.

Have mercy upon me, O Lord, for I am in trouble: mine eye is
consumed with grief, yea, my soul and my belly.

For my life is spent with grief, and my years with sighing: my
strength faileth because of mine iniquity, and my bones are
consumed.

I was a reproach among all mine enemies, but especially among
my neighbors, and a fear to mine acquaintance: they that
did see me without fled from me.

I am forgotten as a dead man out of mind: I am like a broken vessel.

For I have heard the slander of many: fear was on every side:
while they took counsel together against me, they devised
to take away my life.

But I trusted in thee, O Lord: I said, Thou art my God.

My times are in thy hand: deliver me from the hand of mine
enemies, and from them that persecute me.

Make thy face to shine upon thy servant: save me for thy
mercies' sake.

Let me not be ashamed, O Lord; for I have called upon thee: let the wicked be ashamed, and let them be silent in the grave.

Let the lying lips be put to silence; which speak grievous things proudly and contemptuously against the righteous.

Oh how great is thy goodness, which thou hast laid up for them that fear thee; which thou hast wrought for them that trust in thee before the sons of men!

Thou shalt hide them in the secret of thy presence from the pride of man: thou shalt keep them secretly in a pavilion from the strife of tongues.

Blessed be the Lord: for he hath showed me his marvelous kindness in a strong city.

For I said in my haste, I am cut off from before thine eyes: nevertheless thou heardest the voice of my supplications when I cried unto thee.

O love the Lord, all ye his saints: for the Lord preserveth the faithful, and plentifully rewardeth the proud doer.

Be of good courage, and he shall strengthen your heart, all ye that hope in the Lord.

Where do you seek refuge when you are distressed?

Psalm 32

Blessed is he whose transgression is forgiven, whose sin is covered.

Blessed is the man unto whom the Lord imputeth not iniquity, and in whose spirit there is no guile.

When I kept silence, my bones waxed old through my roaring all the day long.

For day and night thy hand was heavy upon me: my moisture is turned into the drought of summer. Selah.

I acknowledged my sin unto thee, and mine iniquity have I not hid. I said, I will confess my transgressions unto the Lord; and thou forgavest the iniquity of my sin. Selah.

For this shall every one that is godly pray unto thee in a time when thou mayest be found: surely in the floods of great waters they shall not come nigh unto him.

Thou art my hiding place; thou shalt preserve me from trouble; thou shalt compass me about with songs of deliverance. Selah.

I will instruct thee and teach thee in the way which thou shalt go: I will guide thee with mine eye.

Be ye not as the horse, or as the mule, which have no understanding: whose mouth must be held in with bit and bridle, lest they come near unto thee.

Many sorrows shall be to the wicked: but he that trusteth in the Lord, mercy shall compass him about.

Be glad in the Lord, and rejoice, ye righteous: and shout for joy, all ye that are upright in heart.

Corrie ten Boom's work with the Dutch underground,
hiding Jewish refugees from Nazis, was dramatized in the book
The Hiding Place, *which takes its title from
the verse "Thou art my hiding place."
Where is your hiding place?*

_____

_____

_____

_____

_____

_____

_____

Psalm 33

Rejoice in the Lord, O ye righteous: for praise is comely for the
upright.

Praise the Lord with harp: sing unto him with the psaltery and
an instrument of ten strings.

Sing unto him a new song; play skilfully with a loud noise.

For the word of the Lord is right; and all his works are done in
truth.

He loveth righteousness and judgment: the earth is full of the
goodness of the Lord.

By the word of the Lord were the heavens made; and all the
host of them by the breath of his mouth.

He gathereth the waters of the sea together as a heap: he layeth
up the depth in storehouses.

Let all the earth fear the Lord: let all the inhabitants of the
world stand in awe of him.

For he spake, and it was done; he commanded, and it stood fast.

The Lord bringeth the counsel of the heathen to nought: he
maketh the devices of the people of none effect.

The counsel of the Lord standeth forever, the thoughts of his
heart to all generations.

Blessed is the nation whose God is the Lord; and the people
whom he hath chosen for his own inheritance.

The Lord looketh from heaven; he beholdeth all the sons of men.

From the place of his habitation he looketh upon all the
inhabitants of the earth.

He fashioneth their hearts alike; he considereth all their works.

There is no king saved by the multitude of a host: a mighty man
is not delivered by much strength.

A horse is a vain thing for safety: neither shall he deliver any by
his great strength.

Behold, the eye of the Lord is upon them that fear him, upon
them that hope in his mercy;

To deliver their soul from death, and to keep them alive in famine.
Our soul waiteth for the Lord: he is our help and our shield.
For our heart shall rejoice in him, because we have trusted in his
    holy name.
Let thy mercy, O Lord, be upon us, according as we hope in thee.

What other phrases, besides "our help and our shield,"
would you use to characterize God?

Psalm 34

I will bless the Lord at all times: his praise shall continually be in my mouth.

My soul shall make her boast in the Lord: the humble shall hear thereof, and be glad.

O magnify the Lord with me, and let us exalt his name together.

I sought the Lord, and he heard me, and delivered me from all my fears.

They looked unto him, and were lightened: and their faces were not ashamed.

This poor man cried, and the Lord heard him, and saved him out of all his troubles.

The angel of the Lord encampeth round about them that fear him, and delivereth them.

O taste and see that the Lord is good: blessed is the man that trusteth in him.

O fear the Lord, ye his saints: for there is no want to them that fear him.

The young lions do lack, and suffer hunger: but they that seek the Lord shall not want any good thing.

Come, ye children, hearken unto me: I will teach you the fear of the Lord.

What man is he that desireth life, and loveth many days, that he may see good?

Keep thy tongue from evil, and thy lips from speaking guile.

Depart from evil, and do good; seek peace, and pursue it.

The eyes of the Lord are upon the righteous, and his ears are open unto their cry.

The face of the Lord is against them that do evil, to cut off the remembrance of them from the earth.

The righteous cry, and the Lord heareth, and delivereth them out of all their troubles.

The Lord is nigh unto them that are of a broken heart; and saveth such as be of a contrite spirit.

Many are the afflictions of the righteous: but the Lord
    delivereth him out of them all.
He keepeth all his bones: not one of them is broken.
Evil shall slay the wicked: and they that hate the righteous shall
    be desolate.
The Lord redeemeth the soul of his servants: and none of them
    that trust in him shall be desolate.

Search for the psalm "Taste and See," and sing along.
What feelings does it evoke in you?

Psalm 35

Plead my cause, O Lord, with them that strive with me: fight against them that fight against me.

Take hold of shield and buckler, and stand up for mine help.

Draw out also the spear, and stop the way against them that persecute me: say unto my soul, I am thy salvation.

Let them be confounded and put to shame that seek after my soul: let them be turned back and brought to confusion that devise my hurt.

Let them be as chaff before the wind: and let the angel of the Lord chase them.

Let their way be dark and slippery: and let the angel of the Lord persecute them.

For without cause have they hid for me their net in a pit, which without cause they have digged for my soul.

Let destruction come upon him at unawares; and let his net that he hath hid catch himself: into that very destruction let him fall.

And my soul shall be joyful in the Lord: it shall rejoice in his salvation.

All my bones shall say, Lord, who is like unto thee, which deliverest the poor from him that is too strong for him, yea, the poor and the needy from him that spoileth him?

False witnesses did rise up; they laid to my charge things that I knew not.

They rewarded me evil for good to the spoiling of my soul.

But as for me, when they were sick, my clothing was sackcloth: I humbled my soul with fasting; and my prayer returned into mine own bosom.

I behaved myself as though he had been my friend or brother: I bowed down heavily, as one that mourneth for his mother.

But in mine adversity they rejoiced, and gathered themselves together: yea, the abjects gathered themselves together against me, and I knew it not; they did tear me, and ceased not:

With hypocritical mockers in feasts, they gnashed upon me with their teeth.

Lord, how long wilt thou look on? rescue my soul from their destructions, my darling from the lions.

I will give thee thanks in the great congregation: I will praise thee among much people.

Let not them that are mine enemies wrongfully rejoice over me: neither let them wink with the eye that hate me without a cause.

For they speak not peace: but they devise deceitful matters against them that are quiet in the land.

Yea, they opened their mouth wide against me, and said, Aha, aha, our eye hath seen it.

This thou hast seen, O Lord: keep not silence: O Lord, be not far from me.

Stir up thyself, and awake to my judgment, even unto my cause, my God and my Lord.

Judge me, O Lord my God, according to thy righteousness; and let them not rejoice over me.

Let them not say in their hearts, Ah, so would we have it: let them not say, We have swallowed him up.

Let them be ashamed and brought to confusion together that rejoice at mine hurt: let them be clothed with shame and dishonor that magnify themselves against me.

Let them shout for joy, and be glad, that favor my righteous cause: yea, let them say continually, Let the Lord be magnified, which hath pleasure in the prosperity of his servant.

And my tongue shall speak of thy righteousness and of thy praise all the day long.

When someone turns against you, do you pray for their destruction, as in this psalm? Can you find forgiveness instead?

Psalm 36

The transgression of the wicked saith within my heart, that
    there is no fear of God before his eyes.
For he flattereth himself in his own eyes, until his iniquity be
    found to be hateful.
The words of his mouth are iniquity and deceit: he hath left off
    to be wise, and to do good.
He deviseth mischief upon his bed; he setteth himself in a way
    that is not good; he abhorreth not evil.
Thy mercy, O Lord, is in the heavens; and thy faithfulness
    reacheth unto the clouds.
Thy righteousness is like the great mountains; thy judgments
    are a great deep: O Lord, thou preservest man and beast.
How excellent is thy loving-kindness, O God! therefore the
    children of men put their trust under the shadow of thy wings.
They shall be abundantly satisfied with the fatness of thy house;
    and thou shalt make them drink of the river of thy pleasures.
For with thee is the fountain of life: in thy light shall we see light.
O continue thy loving-kindness unto them that know thee; and
    thy righteousness to the upright in heart.
Let not the foot of pride come against me, and let not the hand
    of the wicked remove me.
There are the workers of iniquity fallen: they are cast down, and
    shall not be able to rise.

There are two references in this psalm to loving-kindness.
What does that mean to you? Do you find that in your faith?

Psalm 37

Fret not thyself because of evildoers, neither be thou envious
  against the workers of iniquity.
For they shall soon be cut down like the grass, and wither as the
  green herb.
Trust in the Lord, and do good; so shalt thou dwell in the land,
  and verily thou shalt be fed.
Delight thyself also in the Lord; and he shall give thee the
  desires of thine heart.
Commit thy way unto the Lord; trust also in him; and he shall
  bring it to pass.
And he shall bring forth thy righteousness as the light, and thy
  judgment as the noonday.
Rest in the Lord, and wait patiently for him: fret not thyself
  because of him who prospereth in his way, because of the
  man who bringeth wicked devices to pass.
Cease from anger, and forsake wrath: fret not thyself in any wise
  to do evil.
For evildoers shall be cut off: but those that wait upon the Lord,
  they shall inherit the earth.
For yet a little while, and the wicked shall not be: yea, thou
  shalt diligently consider his place, and it shall not be.
But the meek shall inherit the earth; and shall delight
  themselves in the abundance of peace.
The wicked plotteth against the just, and gnasheth upon him
  with his teeth.
The Lord shall laugh at him: for he seeth that his day is coming.
The wicked have drawn out the sword, and have bent their
  bow, to cast down the poor and needy, and to slay such as
  be of upright conversation.
Their sword shall enter into their own heart, and their bows
  shall be broken.
A little that a righteous man hath is better than the riches of
  many wicked.

For the arms of the wicked shall be broken: but the Lord
   upholdeth the righteous.
The Lord knoweth the days of the upright: and their
   inheritance shall be forever.
They shall not be ashamed in the evil time: and in the days of
   famine they shall be satisfied.
But the wicked shall perish, and the enemies of the Lord shall
   be as the fat of lambs: they shall consume; into smoke shall
   they consume away.
The wicked borroweth, and payeth not again: but the righteous
   showeth mercy, and giveth.
For such as be blessed of him shall inherit the earth; and they
   that be cursed of him shall be cut off.
The steps of a good man are ordered by the Lord: and he
   delighteth in his way.
Though he fall, he shall not be utterly cast down: for the Lord
   upholdeth him with his hand.
I have been young, and now am old; yet have I not seen the
   righteous forsaken, nor his seed begging bread.
He is ever merciful, and lendeth; and his seed is blessed.
Depart from evil, and do good; and dwell forevermore.
For the Lord loveth judgment, and forsaketh not his saints; they
   are preserved forever: but the seed of the wicked shall be
   cut off.
The righteous shall inherit the land, and dwell therein forever.
The mouth of the righteous speaketh wisdom, and his tongue
   talketh of judgment.
The law of his God is in his heart; none of his steps shall slide.
The wicked watcheth the righteous, and seeketh to slay him.
The Lord will not leave him in his hand, nor condemn him
   when he is judged.
Wait on the Lord, and keep his way, and he shall exalt thee to
   inherit the land: when the wicked are cut off, thou shalt see it.
I have seen the wicked in great power, and spreading himself
   like a green bay tree.

Yet he passed away, and, lo, he was not: yea, I sought him, but he could not be found.

Mark the perfect man, and behold the upright: for the end of that man is peace.

But the transgressors shall be destroyed together: the end of the wicked shall be cut off.

But the salvation of the righteous is of the Lord: he is their strength in the time of trouble.

And the Lord shall help them, and deliver them: he shall deliver them from the wicked, and save them, because they trust in him.

Will you follow the way of the righteous?
What does that mean in your life?

Psalm 38

O Lord, rebuke me not in thy wrath: neither chasten me in thy
   hot displeasure.

For thine arrows stick fast in me, and thy hand presseth me sore.

There is no soundness in my flesh because of thine anger;
   neither is there any rest in my bones because of my sin.

For mine iniquities are gone over mine head: as a heavy burden
   they are too heavy for me.

My wounds stink and are corrupt because of my foolishness.

I am troubled; I am bowed down greatly; I go mourning all the
   day long.

For my loins are filled with a loathsome disease: and there is no
   soundness in my flesh.

I am feeble and sore broken: I have roared by reason of the
   disquietness of my heart.

Lord, all my desire is before thee; and my groaning is not hid
   from thee.

My heart panteth, my strength faileth me: as for the light of
   mine eyes, it also is gone from me.

My lovers and my friends stand aloof from my sore; and my
   kinsmen stand afar off.

They also that seek after my life lay snares for me; and they that
   seek my hurt speak mischievous things, and imagine deceits
   all the day long.

But I, as a deaf man, heard not; and I was as a dumb man that
   openeth not his mouth.

Thus I was as a man that heareth not, and in whose mouth are
   no reproofs.

For in thee, O Lord, do I hope: thou wilt hear, O Lord my God.

For I said, Hear me, lest otherwise they should rejoice over me:
   when my foot slippeth, they magnify themselves against
   me.

For I am ready to halt, and my sorrow is continually before me.

For I will declare mine iniquity; I will be sorry for my sin.
But mine enemies are lively, and they are strong: and they that
hate me wrongfully are multiplied.
They also that render evil for good are mine adversaries;
because I follow the thing that good is.
Forsake me not, O Lord: O my God, be not far from me.
Make haste to help me, O Lord my salvation.

---

*Have you felt down and broken? How has your faith
helped you find strength during those times?*

Psalm 39

I said, I will take heed to my ways, that I sin not with my
   tongue: I will keep my mouth with a bridle, while the
   wicked is before me.

I was dumb with silence, I held my peace, even from good; and
   my sorrow was stirred.

My heart was hot within me; while I was musing the fire
   burned: then spake I with my tongue,

Lord, make me to know mine end, and the measure of my days,
   what it is; that I may know how frail I am.

Behold, thou hast made my days as a handbreadth; and mine
   age is as nothing before thee: verily every man at his best
   state is altogether vanity. Selah.

Surely every man walketh in a vain show: surely they are
   disquieted in vain: he heapeth up riches, and knoweth not
   who shall gather them.

And now, Lord, what wait I for? my hope is in thee.

Deliver me from all my transgressions: make me not the
   reproach of the foolish.

I was dumb, I opened not my mouth; because thou didst it.

Remove thy stroke away from me: I am consumed by the blow
   of thine hand.

When thou with rebukes dost correct man for iniquity, thou
   makest his beauty to consume away like a moth: surely
   every man is vanity. Selah.

Hear my prayer, O Lord, and give ear unto my cry; hold not
   thy peace at my tears: for I am a stranger with thee, and a
   sojourner, as all my fathers were.

O spare me, that I may recover strength, before I go hence, and
   be no more.

"Here today, gone tomorrow." Mortality is at the forefront of this psalm. How do you feel about *"the measure of my days"*?

Psalm 40

I waited patiently for the Lord; and he inclined unto me, and heard my cry.

He brought me up also out of a horrible pit, out of the miry clay, and set my feet upon a rock, and established my goings.

And he hath put a new song in my mouth, even praise unto our God: many shall see it, and fear, and shall trust in the Lord.

Blessed is that man that maketh the Lord his trust, and respecteth not the proud, nor such as turn aside to lies.

Many, O Lord my God, are thy wonderful works which thou hast done, and thy thoughts which are to us-ward: they cannot be reckoned up in order unto thee: if I would declare and speak of them, they are more than can be numbered.

Sacrifice and offering thou didst not desire; mine ears hast thou opened: burnt offering and sin offering hast thou not required.

Then said I, Lo, I come: in the volume of the book it is written of me,

I delight to do thy will, O my God: yea, thy law is within my heart.

I have preached righteousness in the great congregation: lo, I have not refrained my lips, O Lord, thou knowest.

I have not hid thy righteousness within my heart; I have declared thy faithfulness and thy salvation: I have not concealed thy loving-kindness and thy truth from the great congregation.

Withhold not thou thy tender mercies from me, O Lord: let thy loving-kindness and thy truth continually preserve me.

For innumerable evils have compassed me about: mine iniquities have taken hold upon me, so that I am not able to look up; they are more than the hairs of mine head: therefore my heart faileth me.

Be pleased, O Lord, to deliver me: O Lord, make haste to help me.

Let them be ashamed and confounded together that seek after my soul to destroy it; let them be driven backward and put to shame that wish me evil.

Let them be desolate for a reward of their shame that say unto me, Aha, aha.

Let all those that seek thee rejoice and be glad in thee: let such as love thy salvation say continually, The Lord be magnified.

But I am poor and needy; yet the Lord thinketh upon me: thou art my help and my deliverer; make no tarrying, O my God.

Listen to U2's song "40." Does it feel odd to hear these same words put to music by a contemporary rock band?

Psalm 41

Blessed is he that considereth the poor: the Lord will deliver him in time of trouble.

The Lord will preserve him, and keep him alive; and he shall be blessed upon the earth: and thou wilt not deliver him unto the will of his enemies.

The Lord will strengthen him upon the bed of languishing: thou wilt make all his bed in his sickness.

I said, Lord, be merciful unto me: heal my soul; for I have sinned against thee.

Mine enemies speak evil of me, When shall he die, and his name perish?

And if he come to see me, he speaketh vanity: his heart gathereth iniquity to itself; when he goeth abroad, he telleth it.

All that hate me whisper together against me: against me do they devise my hurt.

An evil disease, say they, cleaveth fast unto him: and now that he lieth he shall rise up no more.

Yea, mine own familiar friend, in whom I trusted, which did eat of my bread, hath lifted up his heel against me.

But thou, O Lord, be merciful unto me, and raise me up, that I may requite them.

By this I know that thou favorest me, because mine enemy doth not triumph over me.

And as for me, thou upholdest me in mine integrity, and settest me before thy face forever.

Blessed be the Lord God of Israel from everlasting, and to everlasting. Amen, and Amen.

This is the last psalm of Book 1.
What kind of reassurance do you gain from it?

_____

_____

_____

_____

_____

_____

_____

_____

_____

_____

Psalm 42

As the hart panteth after the water brooks, so panteth my soul
    after thee, O God.

My soul thirsteth for God, for the living God: when shall I
    come and appear before God?

My tears have been my meat day and night, while they
    continually say unto me, Where is thy God?

When I remember these things, I pour out my soul in me: for I
    had gone with the multitude, I went with them to the house
    of God, with the voice of joy and praise, with a multitude
    that kept holyday.

Why art thou cast down, O my soul? and why art thou
    disquieted in me? hope thou in God: for I shall yet praise
    him for the help of his countenance.

O my God, my soul is cast down within me: therefore will
    I remember thee from the land of Jordan, and of the
    Hermonites, from the hill Mizar.

Deep calleth unto deep at the noise of thy waterspouts: all thy
    waves and thy billows are gone over me.

Yet the Lord will command his loving-kindness in the daytime,
    and in the night his song shall be with me, and my prayer
    unto the God of my life.

I will say unto God my rock, Why hast thou forgotten me? why
    go I mourning because of the oppression of the enemy?

As with a sword in my bones, mine enemies reproach me; while
    they say daily unto me, Where is thy God?

Why art thou cast down, O my soul? and why art thou disquieted
    within me? hope thou in God: for I shall yet praise him, who
    is the health of my countenance, and my God.

Water is a recurring image in this psalm.
What do you make of that?

Psalm 43

Judge me, O God, and plead my cause against an ungodly
    nation: O deliver me from the deceitful and unjust man.
For thou art the God of my strength: why dost thou cast me
    off? why go I mourning because of the oppression of the
    enemy?
O send out thy light and thy truth: let them lead me; let them
    bring me unto thy holy hill, and to thy tabernacles.
Then will I go unto the altar of God, unto God my exceeding
    joy: yea, upon the harp will I praise thee, O God my
    God.
Why art thou cast down, O my soul? and why art thou
    disquieted within me? hope in God: for I shall yet praise
    him, who is the health of my countenance, and my God.

---

*Is God your strength, your exceeding joy, the health of your
countenance? Reflect on what these descriptions mean in your life.*

ʻPsalm 44

We have heard with our ears, O God, our fathers have told us,
what work thou didst in their days, in the times of old.

How thou didst drive out the heathen with thy hand, and
plantedst them; how thou didst afflict the people, and cast
them out.

For they got not the land in possession by their own sword,
neither did their own arm save them: but thy right hand,
and thine arm, and the light of thy countenance, because
thou hadst a favor unto them.

Thou art my King, O God: command deliverances for Jacob.

Through thee will we push down our enemies: through thy
name will we tread them under that rise up against us.

For I will not trust in my bow, neither shall my sword save me.

But thou hast saved us from our enemies, and hast put them to
shame that hated us.

In God we boast all the day long, and praise thy name forever.
Selah.

But thou hast cast off, and put us to shame; and goest not forth
with our armies.

Thou makest us to turn back from the enemy: and they which
hate us spoil for themselves.

Thou hast given us like sheep appointed for meat; and hast
scattered us among the heathen.

Thou sellest thy people for nought, and dost not increase thy
wealth by their price.

Thou makest us a reproach to our neighbors, a scorn and a
derision to them that are round about us.

Thou makest us a byword among the heathen, a shaking of the
head among the people.

My confusion is continually before me, and the shame of my
face hath covered me,

For the voice of him that reproacheth and blasphemeth; by
reason of the enemy and avenger.

All this is come upon us; yet have we not forgotten thee, neither
   have we dealt falsely in thy covenant.

Our heart is not turned back, neither have our steps declined
   from thy way;

Though thou hast sore broken us in the place of dragons, and
   covered us with the shadow of death.

If we have forgotten the name of our God, or stretched out our
   hands to a strange god;

Shall not God search this out? for he knoweth the secrets of the
   heart.

Yea, for thy sake are we killed all the day long; we are counted
   as sheep for the slaughter.

Awake, why sleepest thou, O Lord? arise, cast us not off forever.

Wherefore hidest thou thy face, and forgettest our affliction and
   our oppression?

For our soul is bowed down to the dust: our belly cleaveth unto
   the earth.

Arise for our help, and redeem us for thy mercies' sake.

---

*When have you felt cast off by God? How did you find
your way back to Him?*

Psalm 45

My heart is inditing a good matter: I speak of the things which
I have made touching the King: my tongue is the pen of a
ready writer.

Thou art fairer than the children of men: grace is poured into
thy lips: therefore God hath blessed thee forever.

Gird thy sword upon thy thigh, O most Mighty, with thy glory
and thy majesty.

And in thy majesty ride prosperously, because of truth and
meekness and righteousness; and thy right hand shall teach
thee terrible things.

Thine arrows are sharp in the heart of the King's enemies;
whereby the people fall under thee.

Thy throne, O God, is forever and ever: the sceptre of thy
kingdom is a right sceptre.

Thou lovest righteousness, and hatest wickedness: therefore
God, thy God, hath anointed thee with the oil of gladness
above thy fellows.

All thy garments smell of myrrh, and aloes, and cassia, out of
the ivory palaces, whereby they have made thee glad.

Kings' daughters were among thy honorable women: upon thy
right hand did stand the queen in gold of Ophir.

Hearken, O daughter, and consider, and incline thine ear; forget
also thine own people, and thy father's house;

So shall the King greatly desire thy beauty: for he is thy Lord;
and worship thou him.

And the daughter of Tyre shall be there with a gift; even the
rich among the people shall entreat thy favor.

The King's daughter is all glorious within: her clothing is of
wrought gold.

She shall be brought unto the King in raiment of needlework:
the virgins her companions that follow her shall be brought
unto thee.

With gladness and rejoicing shall they be brought: they shall enter into the King's palace.

Instead of thy fathers shall be thy children, whom thou mayest make princes in all the earth.

I will make thy name to be remembered in all generations: therefore shall the people praise thee forever and ever.

This is known as a wedding song. Who is getting married?
Is this a verse that you would want to have read at your wedding?

Psalm 46

God is our refuge and strength, a very present help in trouble.

Therefore will not we fear, though the earth be removed, and though the mountains be carried into the midst of the sea;

Though the waters thereof roar and be troubled, though the mountains shake with the swelling thereof. Selah.

There is a river, the streams whereof shall make glad the city of God, the holy place of the tabernacles of the Most High.

God is in the midst of her; she shall not be moved: God shall help her, and that right early.

The heathen raged, the kingdoms were moved: he uttered his voice, the earth melted.

The Lord of hosts is with us; the God of Jacob is our refuge. Selah.

Come, behold the works of the Lord, what desolations he hath made in the earth.

He maketh wars to cease unto the end of the earth; he breaketh the bow, and cutteth the spear in sunder; he burneth the chariot in the fire.

Be still, and know that I am God: I will be exalted among the heathen, I will be exalted in the earth.

The Lord of hosts is with us; the God of Jacob is our refuge. Selah.

Sit with this psalm in the morning, carry it with you throughout the day, and pray it before you lie down for the night.

Psalm 47

O clap your hands, all ye people; shout unto God with the
voice of triumph.

For the Lord most high is terrible; he is a great King over all the
earth.

He shall subdue the people under us, and the nations under our
feet.

He shall choose our inheritance for us, the excellency of Jacob
whom he loved. Selah.

God is gone up with a shout, the Lord with the sound of a
trumpet.

Sing praises to God, sing praises: sing praises unto our King,
sing praises.

For God is the King of all the earth: sing ye praises with
understanding.

God reigneth over the heathen: God sitteth upon the throne of
his holiness.

The princes of the people are gathered together, even the
people of the God of Abraham: for the shields of the earth
belong unto God: he is greatly exalted.

---

*Look up other translations of the Bible to glean the meaning of
"For the Lord most high is terrible." Does this resonate with you?*

Psalm 48

Great is the Lord, and greatly to be praised in the city of our
    God, in the mountain of his holiness.
Beautiful for situation, the joy of the whole earth, is mount
    Zion, on the sides of the north, the city of the great King.
God is known in her palaces for a refuge.
For, lo, the kings were assembled, they passed by together.
They saw it, and so they marveled; they were troubled, and
    hasted away.
Fear took hold upon them there, and pain, as of a woman in travail.
Thou breakest the ships of Tarshish with an east wind.
As we have heard, so have we seen in the city of the Lord of hosts,
    in the city of our God: God will establish it forever. Selah.
We have thought of thy loving-kindness, O God, in the midst
    of thy temple.
According to thy name, O God, so is thy praise unto the ends
    of the earth: thy right hand is full of righteousness.
Let mount Zion rejoice, let the daughters of Judah be glad,
    because of thy judgments.
Walk about Zion, and go round about her: tell the towers thereof.
Mark ye well her bulwarks, consider her palaces; that ye may
    tell it to the generation following.
For this God is our God forever and ever: he will be our guide
    even unto death.

Mount Zion is a holy place. What is your holy place?
Picture yourself in that place and reflect on how you feel.

Psalm 49

Hear this, all ye people; give ear, all ye inhabitants of the world:
Both low and high, rich and poor, together.
My mouth shall speak of wisdom; and the meditation of my
    heart shall be of understanding.
I will incline mine ear to a parable: I will open my dark saying
    upon the harp.
Wherefore should I fear in the days of evil, when the iniquity of
    my heels shall compass me about?
They that trust in their wealth, and boast themselves in the
    multitude of their riches;
None of them can by any means redeem his brother, nor give to
    God a ransom for him:
(For the redemption of their soul is precious, and it ceaseth
    forever:)
That he should still live forever, and not see corruption.
For he seeth that wise men die, likewise the fool and the brutish
    person perish, and leave their wealth to others.
Their inward thought is, that their houses shall continue
    forever, and their dwelling places to all generations; they
    call their lands after their own names.
Nevertheless man being in honor abideth not: he is like the
    beasts that perish.
This their way is their folly: yet their posterity approve their
    sayings. Selah.
Like sheep they are laid in the grave; death shall feed on them;
    and the upright shall have dominion over them in the
    morning; and their beauty shall consume in the grave from
    their dwelling.
But God will redeem my soul from the power of the grave: for
    he shall receive me. Selah.
Be not thou afraid when one is made rich, when the glory of his
    house is increased;

For when he dieth he shall carry nothing away: his glory shall
    not descend after him.
Though while he lived he blessed his soul, (and men will praise
    thee, when thou doest well to thyself,)
He shall go to the generation of his fathers; they shall never see
    light.
Man that is in honor, and understandeth not, is like the beasts
    that perish.

Man "is like the beasts that perish" is repeated twice in this psalm.
Why do you think that is?

Psalm 50

The mighty God, even the Lord, hath spoken, and called
 the earth from the rising of the sun unto the going down
 thereof.
Out of Zion, the perfection of beauty, God hath shined.
Our God shall come, and shall not keep silence: a fire shall
 devour before him, and it shall be very tempestuous round
 about him.
He shall call to the heavens from above, and to the earth, that
 he may judge his people.
Gather my saints together unto me; those that have made a
 covenant with me by sacrifice.
And the heavens shall declare his righteousness: for God is
 judge himself. Selah.
Hear, O my people, and I will speak; O Israel, and I will testify
 against thee: I am God, even thy God.
I will not reprove thee for thy sacrifices or thy burnt offerings,
 to have been continually before me.
I will take no bullock out of thy house, nor he goats out of thy
 folds:
For every beast of the forest is mine, and the cattle upon a
 thousand hills.
I know all the fowls of the mountains: and the wild beasts of the
 field are mine.
If I were hungry, I would not tell thee: for the world is mine,
 and the fulness thereof.
Will I eat the flesh of bulls, or drink the blood of goats?
Offer unto God thanksgiving; and pay thy vows unto the Most
 High:
And call upon me in the day of trouble: I will deliver thee, and
 thou shalt glorify me.

But unto the wicked God saith, What hast thou to do to declare my statutes, or that thou shouldest take my covenant in thy mouth?

Seeing thou hatest instruction, and castest my words behind thee.

When thou sawest a thief, then thou consentedst with him, and hast been partaker with adulterers.

Thou givest thy mouth to evil, and thy tongue frameth deceit.

Thou sittest and speakest against thy brother; thou slanderest thine own mother's son.

These things hast thou done, and I kept silence; thou thoughtest that I was altogether such a one as thyself: but I will reprove thee, and set them in order before thine eyes.

Now consider this, ye that forget God, lest I tear you in pieces, and there be none to deliver.

Whoso offereth praise glorifieth me: and to him that ordereth his conversation aright will I show the salvation of God.

How do you feel about God judging you? Consider this when you find yourself judging others.

Psalm 51

Have mercy upon me, O God, according to thy loving-
kindness: according unto the multitude of thy tender
mercies blot out my transgressions.

Wash me thoroughly from mine iniquity, and cleanse me from
my sin.

For I acknowledge my transgressions: and my sin is ever before
me.

Against thee, thee only, have I sinned, and done this evil in thy
sight: that thou mightest be justified when thou speakest,
and be clear when thou judgest.

Behold, I was shapen in iniquity; and in sin did my mother
conceive me.

Behold, thou desirest truth in the inward parts: and in the
hidden part thou shalt make me to know wisdom.

Purge me with hyssop, and I shall be clean: wash me, and I shall
be whiter than snow.

Make me to hear joy and gladness; that the bones which thou
hast broken may rejoice.

Hide thy face from my sins, and blot out all mine iniquities.

Create in me a clean heart, O God; and renew a right spirit
within me.

Cast me not away from thy presence; and take not thy Holy
Spirit from me.

Restore unto me the joy of thy salvation; and uphold me with
thy free Spirit.

Then will I teach transgressors thy ways; and sinners shall be
converted unto thee.

Deliver me from bloodguiltiness, O God, thou God of
my salvation: and my tongue shall sing aloud of thy
righteousness.

O Lord, open thou my lips; and my mouth shall show forth thy
praise.

For thou desirest not sacrifice; else would I give it: thou
   delightest not in burnt offering.
The sacrifices of God are a broken spirit: a broken and a
   contrite heart, O God, thou wilt not despise.
Do good in thy good pleasure unto Zion: build thou the walls
   of Jerusalem.
Then shalt thou be pleased with the sacrifices of righteousness,
   with burnt offering and whole burnt offering: then shall
   they offer bullocks upon thine altar.

*David committed adultery with Uriah's wife, Bathsheba.
This is David's prayer of repentance. Write one of your own.*

Psalm 52

Why boastest thou thyself in mischief, O mighty man? the
goodness of God endureth continually.

Thy tongue deviseth mischiefs; like a sharp razor, working
deceitfully.

Thou lovest evil more than good; and lying rather than to speak
righteousness. Selah.

Thou lovest all devouring words, O thou deceitful tongue.

God shall likewise destroy thee forever, he shall take thee away,
and pluck thee out of thy dwelling place, and root thee out
of the land of the living. Selah.

The righteous also shall see, and fear, and shall laugh at him:

Lo, this is the man that made not God his strength; but trusted
in the abundance of his riches, and strengthened himself in
his wickedness.

But I am like a green olive tree in the house of God: I trust in
the mercy of God forever and ever.

I will praise thee forever, because thou hast done it: and I will
wait on thy name; for it is good before thy saints.

*What does this psalm tell you if you trust
in your own self and not in God?*

'Psalm 53

The fool hath said in his heart, There is no God. Corrupt are
  they, and have done abominable iniquity: there is none that
  doeth good.
God looked down from heaven upon the children of men, to see
  if there were any that did understand, that did seek God.
Every one of them is gone back: they are altogether become
  filthy; there is none that doeth good, no, not one.
Have the workers of iniquity no knowledge? who eat up my
  people as they eat bread: they have not called upon God.
There were they in great fear, where no fear was: for God hath
  scattered the bones of him that encampeth against thee:
  thou hast put them to shame, because God hath despised
  them.
Oh that the salvation of Israel were come out of Zion! When
  God bringeth back the captivity of his people, Jacob shall
  rejoice, and Israel shall be glad.

*Is there a God? How do you retain
your faith when it is challenged?*

Psalm 54

Save me, O God, by thy name, and judge me by thy strength.
Hear my prayer, O God; give ear to the words of my mouth.
For strangers are risen up against me, and oppressors seek after
my soul: they have not set God before them. Selah.
Behold, God is mine helper: the Lord is with them that uphold
my soul.
He shall reward evil unto mine enemies: cut them off in thy
truth.
I will freely sacrifice unto thee: I will praise thy name, O Lord;
for it is good.
For he hath delivered me out of all trouble: and mine eye hath
seen his desire upon mine enemies.

---

*Listen to a recording of "Save Me by Your Name,
O God" (a timeless a cappella project performed by Vocal Tapestry).
Allow the music to dwell in you today.*

Psalm 55

Give ear to my prayer, O God; and hide not thyself from my
    supplication.

Attend unto me, and hear me: I mourn in my complaint, and
    make a noise;

Because of the voice of the enemy, because of the oppression
    of the wicked: for they cast iniquity upon me, and in wrath
    they hate me.

My heart is sore pained within me: and the terrors of death are
    fallen upon me.

Fearfulness and trembling are come upon me, and horror hath
    overwhelmed me.

And I said, Oh that I had wings like a dove! for then would I fly
    away, and be at rest.

Lo, then would I wander far off, and remain in the wilderness.
    Selah.

I would hasten my escape from the windy storm and tempest.

Destroy, O Lord, and divide their tongues: for I have seen
    violence and strife in the city.

Day and night they go about it upon the walls thereof: mischief
    also and sorrow are in the midst of it.

Wickedness is in the midst thereof: deceit and guile depart not
    from her streets.

For it was not an enemy that reproached me; then I could have
    borne it: neither was it he that hated me that did magnify
    himself against me; then I would have hid myself from him:

But it was thou, a man mine equal, my guide, and mine
    acquaintance.

We took sweet counsel together, and walked unto the house of
    God in company.

Let death seize upon them, and let them go down quick into
    hell: for wickedness is in their dwellings, and among them.

As for me, I will call upon God; and the Lord shall save me.

Evening, and morning, and at noon, will I pray, and cry aloud:
and he shall hear my voice.

He hath delivered my soul in peace from the battle that was
against me: for there were many with me.

God shall hear, and afflict them, even he that abideth of old.
Selah. Because they have no changes, therefore they fear
not God.

He hath put forth his hands against such as be at peace with
him: he hath broken his covenant.

The words of his mouth were smoother than butter, but war was
in his heart: his words were softer than oil, yet were they
drawn swords.

Cast thy burden upon the Lord, and he shall sustain thee: he
shall never suffer the righteous to be moved.

But thou, O God, shalt bring them down into the pit of
destruction: bloody and deceitful men shall not live out half
their days; but I will trust in thee.

Think about a time when you were betrayed.
What kind of prayer did you pray?

_____

_____

_____

_____

_____

Psalm 56

Be merciful unto me, O God: for man would swallow me up; he
fighting daily oppresseth me.

Mine enemies would daily swallow me up: for they be many
that fight against me, O thou Most High.

What time I am afraid, I will trust in thee.

In God I will praise his word, in God I have put my trust; I will
not fear what flesh can do unto me.

Every day they wrest my words: all their thoughts are against
me for evil.

They gather themselves together, they hide themselves, they
mark my steps, when they wait for my soul.

Shall they escape by iniquity? in thine anger cast down the
people, O God.

Thou tellest my wanderings: put thou my tears into thy bottle:
are they not in thy book?

When I cry unto thee, then shall mine enemies turn back: this I
know; for God is for me.

In God will I praise his word: in the Lord will I praise his word.

In God have I put my trust: I will not be afraid what man can do
unto me.

Thy vows are upon me, O God: I will render praises unto thee.

For thou hast delivered my soul from death: wilt not thou
deliver my feet from falling, that I may walk before God in
the light of the living?

When you feel afraid or threatened, how do you express it?
Do you turn to God for comfort?

_____

_____

_____

_____

_____

_____

_____

_____

Psalm 57

Be merciful unto me, O God, be merciful unto me: for my soul
trusteth in thee: yea, in the shadow of thy wings will I make
my refuge, until these calamities be overpast.

I will cry unto God most high; unto God that performeth all
things for me.

He shall send from heaven, and save me from the reproach of
him that would swallow me up. Selah. God shall send forth
his mercy and his truth.

My soul is among lions: and I lie even among them that are set
on fire, even the sons of men, whose teeth are spears and
arrows, and their tongue a sharp sword.

Be thou exalted, O God, above the heavens; let thy glory be
above all the earth.

They have prepared a net for my steps; my soul is bowed down:
they have digged a pit before me, into the midst whereof
they are fallen themselves. Selah.

My heart is fixed, O God, my heart is fixed: I will sing and give
praise.

Awake up, my glory; awake, psaltery and harp: I myself will
awake early.

I will praise thee, O Lord among the people: I will sing unto
thee among the nations.

For thy mercy is great unto the heavens, and thy truth unto the
clouds.

Be thou exalted, O God, above the heavens: let thy glory be
above all the earth.

Listen to Abby and Zach Vestnys's original rendition of this prayer for God's mercy. Reflect on how it makes you feel.

Psalm 58

Do ye indeed speak righteousness, O congregation? do ye judge
uprightly, O ye sons of men?

Yea, in heart ye work wickedness; ye weigh the violence of your
hands in the earth.

The wicked are estranged from the womb: they go astray as
soon as they be born, speaking lies.

Their poison is like the poison of a serpent: they are like the
deaf adder that stoppeth her ear;

Which will not hearken to the voice of charmers, charming
never so wisely.

Break their teeth, O God, in their mouth: break out the great
teeth of the young lions, O Lord.

Let them melt away as waters which run continually: when he
bendeth his bow to shoot his arrows, let them be as cut in
pieces.

As a snail which melteth, let every one of them pass away: like
the untimely birth of a woman, that they may not see the
sun.

Before your pots can feel the thorns, he shall take them away as
with a whirlwind, both living, and in his wrath.

The righteous shall rejoice when he seeth the vengeance: he
shall wash his feet in the blood of the wicked.

So that a man shall say, Verily there is a reward for the
righteous: verily he is a God that judgeth in the earth.

How do you feel about God breaking the teeth
of the wicked and cutting the wicked in pieces?
Do you read this literally or metaphorically?

Psalm 59

Deliver me from mine enemies, O my God: defend me from
them that rise up against me.

Deliver me from the workers of iniquity, and save me from
bloody men.

For, lo, they lie in wait for my soul: the mighty are gathered
against me; not for my transgression, nor for my sin,
O Lord.

They run and prepare themselves without my fault: awake to
help me, and behold.

Thou therefore, O Lord God of hosts, the God of Israel, awake
to visit all the heathen: be not merciful to any wicked
transgressors. Selah.

They return at evening: they make a noise like a dog, and go
round about the city.

Behold, they belch out with their mouth: swords are in their
lips: for who, say they, doth hear?

But thou, O Lord, shalt laugh at them; thou shalt have all the
heathen in derision.

Because of his strength will I wait upon thee: for God is my
defense.

The God of my mercy shall prevent me: God shall let me see
my desire upon mine enemies.

Slay them not, lest my people forget: scatter them by thy
power; and bring them down, O Lord our shield.

For the sin of their mouth and the words of their lips let them
even be taken in their pride: and for cursing and lying
which they speak.

Consume them in wrath, consume them, that they may not be:
and let them know that God ruleth in Jacob unto the ends
of the earth. Selah.

And at evening let them return; and let them make a noise like a
dog, and go round about the city.

Let them wander up and down for meat, and grudge if they be
   not satisfied.
But I will sing of thy power; yea, I will sing aloud of thy mercy
   in the morning: for thou hast been my defense and refuge
   in the day of my trouble.
Unto thee, O my strength, will I sing: for God is my defense,
   and the God of my mercy.

---

*What kind of song would you sing to God for delivery
and defense from your enemy?*

ˈPsalm 60

O God, thou hast cast us off, thou hast scattered us, thou hast
    been displeased; O turn thyself to us again.

Thou hast made the earth to tremble; thou hast broken it: heal
    the breaches thereof; for it shaketh.

Thou hast showed thy people hard things: thou hast made us to
    drink the wine of astonishment.

Thou hast given a banner to them that fear thee, that it may be
    displayed because of the truth. Selah.

That thy beloved may be delivered; save with thy right hand,
    and hear me.

God hath spoken in his holiness; I will rejoice, I will divide
    Shechem, and mete out the valley of Succoth.

Gilead is mine, and Manasseh is mine; Ephraim also is the
    strength of mine head; Judah is my lawgiver;

Moab is my washpot; over Edom will I cast out my shoe:
    Philistia, triumph thou because of me.

Who will bring me into the strong city? who will lead me into
    Edom?

Wilt not thou, O God, which hadst cast us off? and thou,
    O God, which didst not go out with our armies?

Give us help from trouble: for vain is the help of man.

Through God we shall do valiantly: for he it is that shall tread
    down our enemies.

---

*Locate these ancient places on a globe or map: Shechem, Succoth,
Gilead, Manasseh, Ephraim, Judah, Moab, Edom, Philistia. Do
you feel that your life is connected to these places in any way?*

Psalm 61

Hear my cry, O God; attend unto my prayer.

From the end of the earth will I cry unto thee, when my heart is overwhelmed: lead me to the rock that is higher than I.

For thou hast been a shelter for me, and a strong tower from the enemy.

I will abide in thy tabernacle forever: I will trust in the covert of thy wings. Selah.

For thou, O God, hast heard my vows: thou hast given me the heritage of those that fear thy name.

Thou wilt prolong the king's life: and his years as many generations.

He shall abide before God forever: O prepare mercy and truth, which may preserve him.

So will I sing praise unto thy name forever, that I may daily perform my vows.

What do you think about this psalm being called a "prayer of an exile"? Have you ever felt exiled?

Psalm 62

Truly my soul waiteth upon God: from him cometh my
    salvation.

He only is my rock and my salvation; he is my defense; I shall
    not be greatly moved.

How long will ye imagine mischief against a man? ye shall
    be slain all of you: as a bowing wall shall ye be, and as a
    tottering fence.

They only consult to cast him down from his excellency: they
    delight in lies: they bless with their mouth, but they curse
    inwardly. Selah.

My soul, wait thou only upon God; for my expectation is from
    him.

He only is my rock and my salvation: he is my defense; I shall
    not be moved.

In God is my salvation and my glory: the rock of my strength,
    and my refuge, is in God.

Trust in him at all times; ye people, pour out your heart before
    him: God is a refuge for us. Selah.

Surely men of low degree are vanity, and men of high degree
    are a lie: to be laid in the balance, they are altogether
    lighter than vanity.

Trust not in oppression, and become not vain in robbery: if
    riches increase, set not your heart upon them.

God hath spoken once; twice have I heard this; that power
    belongeth unto God.

Also unto thee, O Lord, belongeth mercy: for thou renderest to
    every man according to his work.

The Book of Common Prayer suggests reading this on the morning of the twelfth day of the month. Why do you think that timing is suggested?

ˈPsalm 63

O God, thou art my God; early will I seek thee: my soul
    thirsteth for thee, my flesh longeth for thee in a dry and
    thirsty land, where no water is;
To see thy power and thy glory, so as I have seen thee in the
    sanctuary.
Because thy loving-kindness is better than life, my lips shall
    praise thee.
Thus will I bless thee while I live: I will lift up my hands in thy
    name.
My soul shall be satisfied as with marrow and fatness; and my
    mouth shall praise thee with joyful lips:
When I remember thee upon my bed, and meditate on thee in
    the night watches.
Because thou hast been my help, therefore in the shadow of thy
    wings will I rejoice.
My soul followeth hard after thee: thy right hand upholdeth
    me.
But those that seek my soul, to destroy it, shall go into the
    lower parts of the earth.
They shall fall by the sword: they shall be a portion for foxes.
But the king shall rejoice in God; every one that sweareth by
    him shall glory: but the mouth of them that speak lies shall
    be stopped.

---

*This psalm is said to have been written when David was in the
Judean wilderness. Imagine yourself there, with him,
as you say this prayer out loud.*

Psalm 64

Hear my voice, O God, in my prayer: preserve my life from fear
    of the enemy.

Hide me from the secret counsel of the wicked; from the
    insurrection of the workers of iniquity:

Who whet their tongue like a sword, and bend their bows to
    shoot their arrows, even bitter words:

That they may shoot in secret at the perfect: suddenly do they
    shoot at him, and fear not.

They encourage themselves in an evil matter: they commune of
    laying snares privily; they say, Who shall see them?

They search out iniquities; they accomplish a diligent search:
    both the inward thought of every one of them, and the
    heart, is deep.

But God shall shoot at them with an arrow; suddenly shall they
    be wounded.

So they shall make their own tongue to fall upon themselves: all
    that see them shall flee away.

And all men shall fear, and shall declare the work of God; for
    they shall wisely consider of his doing.

The righteous shall be glad in the Lord, and shall trust in him;
    and all the upright in heart shall glory.

*Does the King James Version speak to you, or do you find a need
for a more contemporary translation?*

Psalm 65

Praise waiteth for thee, O God, in Zion: and unto thee shall the
vow be performed.

O thou that hearest prayer, unto thee shall all flesh come.

Iniquities prevail against me: as for our transgressions, thou shalt
purge them away.

Blessed is the man whom thou choosest, and causest to
approach unto thee, that he may dwell in thy courts: we
shall be satisfied with the goodness of thy house, even of
thy holy temple.

By terrible things in righteousness wilt thou answer us, O God
of our salvation; who art the confidence of all the ends of
the earth, and of them that are afar off upon the sea:

Which by his strength setteth fast the mountains: being girded
with power:

Which stilleth the noise of the seas, the noise of their waves,
and the tumult of the people.

They also that dwell in the uttermost parts are afraid at thy
tokens: thou makest the outgoings of the morning and
evening to rejoice.

Thou visitest the earth, and waterest it: thou greatly enrichest it
with the river of God, which is full of water: thou preparest
them corn, when thou hast so provided for it.

Thou waterest the ridges thereof abundantly: thou settlest the
furrows thereof: thou makest it soft with showers: thou
blessest the springing thereof.

Thou crownest the year with thy goodness; and thy paths drop
fatness.

They drop upon the pastures of the wilderness: and the little
hills rejoice on every side.
The pastures are clothed with flocks; the valleys also are
covered over with corn; they shout for joy, they also sing.

How do the images of nature in this psalm make you feel?
Do you find comfort in nature?

Psalm 66

Make a joyful noise unto God, all ye lands:

Sing forth the honor of his name: make his praise glorious.

Say unto God, How terrible art thou in thy works! through
the greatness of thy power shall thine enemies submit
themselves unto thee.

All the earth shall worship thee, and shall sing unto thee; they
shall sing to thy name. Selah.

Come and see the works of God: he is terrible in his doing
toward the children of men.

He turned the sea into dry land: they went through the flood on
foot: there did we rejoice in him.

He ruleth by his power forever; his eyes behold the nations: let
not the rebellious exalt themselves. Selah.

O bless our God, ye people, and make the voice of his praise to
be heard:

Which holdeth our soul in life, and suffereth not our feet to be
moved.

For thou, O God, hast proved us: thou hast tried us, as silver is
tried.

Thou broughtest us into the net; thou laidst affliction upon our
loins.

Thou hast caused men to ride over our heads; we went through
fire and through water: but thou broughtest us out into a
wealthy place.

I will go into thy house with burnt offerings: I will pay thee my
vows,

Which my lips have uttered, and my mouth hath spoken, when
I was in trouble.

I will offer unto thee burnt sacrifices of fatlings, with the
incense of rams: I will offer bullocks with goats. Selah.

Come and hear, all ye that fear God, and I will declare what he
hath done for my soul.

I cried unto him with my mouth, and he was extolled with my
tongue.
If I regard iniquity in my heart, the Lord will not hear me:
But verily God hath heard me; he hath attended to the voice of
my prayer.
Blessed be God, which hath not turned away my prayer, nor his
mercy from me.

What does your "joyful noise unto God" sound like?

Psalm 67

God be merciful unto us, and bless us; and cause his face to
shine upon us; Selah.
That thy way may be known upon earth, thy saving health
among all nations.
Let the people praise thee, O God; let all the people praise
thee.
O let the nations be glad and sing for joy: for thou shalt judge
the people righteously, and govern the nations upon earth.
Selah.
Let the people praise thee, O God; let all the people praise
thee.
Then shall the earth yield her increase; and God, even our own
God, shall bless us.
God shall bless us; and all the ends of the earth shall fear him.

Have you experienced God's mercy in your life?
What did that look like? How did it feel?

Psalm 68

Let God arise, let his enemies be scattered: let them also that
hate him flee before him.

As smoke is driven away, so drive them away: as wax melteth
before the fire, so let the wicked perish at the presence of
God.

But let the righteous be glad; let them rejoice before God: yea,
let them exceedingly rejoice.

Sing unto God, sing praises to his name: extol him that rideth
upon the heavens by his name Jah, and rejoice before him.

A father of the fatherless, and a judge of the widows, is God in
his holy habitation.

God setteth the solitary in families: he bringeth out those which
are bound with chains: but the rebellious dwell in a dry
land.

O God, when thou wentest forth before thy people, when thou
didst march through the wilderness; Selah:

The earth shook, the heavens also dropped at the presence of
God: even Sinai itself was moved at the presence of God,
the God of Israel.

Thou, O God, didst send a plentiful rain, whereby thou didst
confirm thine inheritance, when it was weary.

Thy congregation hath dwelt therein: thou, O God, hast
prepared of thy goodness for the poor.

The Lord gave the word: great was the company of those that
published it.

Kings of armies did flee apace: and she that tarried at home
divided the spoil.

Though ye have lain among the pots, yet shall ye be as the
wings of a dove covered with silver, and her feathers with
yellow gold.

When the Almighty scattered kings in it, it was white as snow
in Salmon.

The hill of God is as the hill of Bashan; a high hill as the hill of Bashan.

Why leap ye, ye high hills? this is the hill which God desireth to dwell in; yea, the Lord will dwell in it forever.

The chariots of God are twenty thousand, even thousands of angels: the Lord is among them, as in Sinai, in the holy place.

Thou hast ascended on high, thou hast led captivity captive: thou hast received gifts for men; yea, for the rebellious also, that the Lord God might dwell among them.

Blessed be the Lord, who daily loadeth us with benefits, even the God of our salvation. Selah.

He that is our God is the God of salvation; and unto God the Lord belong the issues from death.

But God shall wound the head of his enemies, and the hairy scalp of such a one as goeth on still in his trespasses.

The Lord said, I will bring again from Bashan, I will bring my people again from the depths of the sea:

That thy foot may be dipped in the blood of thine enemies, and the tongue of thy dogs in the same.

They have seen thy goings, O God; even the goings of my God, my King, in the sanctuary.

The singers went before, the players on instruments followed after; among them were the damsels playing with timbrels.

Bless ye God in the congregations, even the Lord, from the fountain of Israel.

There is little Benjamin with their ruler, the princes of Judah and their council, the princes of Zebulun, and the princes of Naphtali.

Thy God hath commanded thy strength: strengthen, O God, that which thou hast wrought for us.

Because of thy temple at Jerusalem shall kings bring presents unto thee.

Rebuke the company of spearmen, the multitude of the bulls, with the calves of the people, till every one submit himself with pieces of silver: scatter thou the people that delight in war.

Princes shall come out of Egypt; Ethiopia shall soon stretch out her hands unto God.

Sing unto God, ye kingdoms of the earth; O sing praises unto the Lord; Selah:

To him that rideth upon the heavens of heavens, which were of old; lo, he doth send out his voice, and that a mighty voice.

Ascribe ye strength unto God: his excellency is over Israel, and his strength is in the clouds.

O God, thou art terrible out of thy holy places: the God of Israel is he that giveth strength and power unto his people. Blessed be God.

This psalm talks about God delivering peace to His people. How do you reconcile that with all of the conflict in the world today?

Psalm 69

Save me, O God; for the waters are come in unto my soul.

I sink in deep mire, where there is no standing: I am come into deep waters, where the floods overflow me.

I am weary of my crying: my throat is dried: mine eyes fail while I wait for my God.

They that hate me without a cause are more than the hairs of mine head: they that would destroy me, being mine enemies wrongfully, are mighty: then I restored that which I took not away.

O God, thou knowest my foolishness; and my sins are not hid from thee.

Let not them that wait on thee, O Lord God of hosts, be ashamed for my sake: let not those that seek thee be confounded for my sake, O God of Israel.

Because for thy sake I have borne reproach; shame hath covered my face.

I am become a stranger unto my brethren, and an alien unto my mother's children.

For the zeal of thine house hath eaten me up; and the reproaches of them that reproached thee are fallen upon me.

When I wept, and chastened my soul with fasting, that was to my reproach.

I made sackcloth also my garment; and I became a proverb to them.

They that sit in the gate speak against me; and I was the song of the drunkards.

But as for me, my prayer is unto thee, O Lord, in an acceptable time: O God, in the multitude of thy mercy hear me, in the truth of thy salvation.

Deliver me out of the mire, and let me not sink: let me be delivered from them that hate me, and out of the deep waters.

Let not the waterflood overflow me, neither let the deep
swallow me up, and let not the pit shut her mouth upon me.

Hear me, O Lord; for thy loving-kindness is good: turn unto me
according to the multitude of thy tender mercies.

And hide not thy face from thy servant; for I am in trouble: hear
me speedily.

Draw nigh unto my soul, and redeem it: deliver me because of
mine enemies.

Thou hast known my reproach, and my shame, and my
dishonor: mine adversaries are all before thee.

Reproach hath broken my heart; and I am full of heaviness: and
I looked for some to take pity, but there was none; and for
comforters, but I found none.

They gave me also gall for my meat; and in my thirst they gave
me vinegar to drink.

Let their table become a snare before them: and that which
should have been for their welfare, let it become a trap.

Let their eyes be darkened, that they see not; and make their
loins continually to shake.

Pour out thine indignation upon them, and let thy wrathful
anger take hold of them.

Let their habitation be desolate; and let none dwell in their
tents.

For they persecute him whom thou hast smitten; and they talk
to the grief of those whom thou hast wounded.

Add iniquity unto their iniquity: and let them not come into thy
righteousness.

Let them be blotted out of the book of the living, and not be
written with the righteous.

But I am poor and sorrowful: let thy salvation, O God, set me
up on high.

I will praise the name of God with a song, and will magnify him
with thanksgiving.

This also shall please the Lord better than an ox or bullock that hath horns and hoofs.

The humble shall see this, and be glad: and your heart shall live that seek God.

For the Lord heareth the poor, and despiseth not his prisoners.

Let the heaven and earth praise him, the seas, and every thing that moveth therein.

For God will save Zion, and will build the cities of Judah: that they may dwell there, and have it in possession.

The seed also of his servants shall inherit it: and they that love his name shall dwell therein.

Reflect on these phrases: "I became a proverb to them," "I was the song of the drunkards."

Psalm 70

Make haste, O God, to deliver me; make haste to help me,
    O Lord.
Let them be ashamed and confounded that seek after my soul:
    let them be turned backward, and put to confusion, that
    desire my hurt.
Let them be turned back for a reward of their shame that say,
    Aha, aha.
Let all those that seek thee rejoice and be glad in thee: and
    let such as love thy salvation say continually, Let God be
    magnified.
But I am poor and needy; make haste unto me, O God: thou art
    my help and my deliverer; O Lord, make no tarrying.

What would your petition be to God right now?
What do you need from Him?

Psalm 71

In thee, O Lord, do I put my trust: let me never be put to
confusion.

Deliver me in thy righteousness, and cause me to escape: incline
thine ear unto me, and save me.

Be thou my strong habitation, whereunto I may continually
resort: thou hast given commandment to save me; for thou
art my rock and my fortress.

Deliver me, O my God, out of the hand of the wicked, out of
the hand of the unrighteous and cruel man.

For thou art my hope, O Lord God: thou art my trust from my
youth.

By thee have I been holden up from the womb: thou art he
that took me out of my mother's bowels: my praise shall be
continually of thee.

I am as a wonder unto many; but thou art my strong refuge.

Let my mouth be filled with thy praise and with thy honor all
the day.

Cast me not off in the time of old age; forsake me not when my
strength faileth.

For mine enemies speak against me; and they that lay wait for
my soul take counsel together,

Saying, God hath forsaken him: persecute and take him; for
there is none to deliver him.

O God, be not far from me: O my God, make haste for my
help.

Let them be confounded and consumed that are adversaries to
my soul; let them be covered with reproach and dishonor
that seek my hurt.

But I will hope continually, and will yet praise thee more and
more.

My mouth shall show forth thy righteousness and thy salvation
all the day; for I know not the numbers thereof.

I will go in the strength of the Lord God: I will make mention
of thy righteousness, even of thine only.
O God, thou hast taught me from my youth: and hitherto have
I declared thy wondrous works.
Now also when I am old and grayheaded, O God, forsake me
not; until I have showed thy strength unto this generation,
and thy power to every one that is to come.
Thy righteousness also, O God, is very high, who hast done
great things: O God, who is like unto thee!
Thou, which hast showed me great and sore troubles, shalt
quicken me again, and shalt bring me up again from the
depths of the earth.
Thou shalt increase my greatness, and comfort me on every
side.
I will also praise thee with the psaltery, even thy truth, O my
God: unto thee will I sing with the harp, O thou Holy One
of Israel.
My lips shall greatly rejoice when I sing unto thee; and my soul,
which thou hast redeemed.
My tongue also shall talk of thy righteousness all the day long:
for they are confounded, for they are brought unto shame,
that seek my hurt.

---

*Do you relate to this prayer from someone who is
"old and grayheaded"?*

Psalm 72

Give the king thy judgments, O God, and thy righteousness
    unto the king's son.

He shall judge thy people with righteousness, and thy poor
    with judgment.

The mountains shall bring peace to the people, and the little
    hills, by righteousness.

He shall judge the poor of the people, he shall save the children
    of the needy, and shall break in pieces the oppressor.

They shall fear thee as long as the sun and moon endure,
    throughout all generations.

He shall come down like rain upon the mown grass: as showers
    that water the earth.

In his days shall the righteous flourish; and abundance of peace
    so long as the moon endureth.

He shall have dominion also from sea to sea, and from the river
    unto the ends of the earth.

They that dwell in the wilderness shall bow before him; and his
    enemies shall lick the dust.

The kings of Tarshish and of the isles shall bring presents: the
    kings of Sheba and Seba shall offer gifts.

Yea, all kings shall fall down before him: all nations shall serve
    him.

For he shall deliver the needy when he crieth; the poor also,
    and him that hath no helper.

He shall spare the poor and needy, and shall save the souls of
    the needy.

He shall redeem their soul from deceit and violence: and
    precious shall their blood be in his sight.

And he shall live, and to him shall be given of the gold of
    Sheba: prayer also shall be made for him continually; and
    daily shall he be praised.

There shall be a handful of corn in the earth upon the top of the
mountains; the fruit thereof shall shake like Lebanon: and
they of the city shall flourish like grass of the earth.
His name shall endure forever: his name shall be continued as
long as the sun: and men shall be blessed in him: all nations
shall call him blessed.
Blessed be the Lord God, the God of Israel, who only doeth
wondrous things.
And blessed be his glorious name forever: and let the whole
earth be filled with his glory. Amen, and Amen.
The prayers of David the son of Jesse are ended.

*This is the last psalm of Book 2. Find different hymns
inspired by it, and listen to them.*

Psalm 73

Truly God is good to Israel, even to such as are of a clean heart.

But as for me, my feet were almost gone; my steps had well-nigh slipped.

For I was envious at the foolish, when I saw the prosperity of the wicked.

For there are no bands in their death: but their strength is firm.

They are not in trouble as other men; neither are they plagued like other men.

Therefore pride compasseth them about as a chain; violence covereth them as a garment.

Their eyes stand out with fatness: they have more than heart could wish.

They are corrupt, and speak wickedly concerning oppression: they speak loftily.

They set their mouth against the heavens, and their tongue walketh through the earth.

Therefore his people return hither: and waters of a full cup are wrung out to them.

And they say, How doth God know? and is there knowledge in the Most High?

Behold, these are the ungodly, who prosper in the world; they increase in riches.

Verily I have cleansed my heart in vain, and washed my hands in innocency.

For all the day long have I been plagued, and chastened every morning.

If I say, I will speak thus; behold, I should offend against the generation of thy children.

When I thought to know this, it was too painful for me;

Until I went into the sanctuary of God; then understood I their end.

Surely thou didst set them in slippery places: thou castedst them down into destruction.

How are they brought into desolation, as in a moment! they are
utterly consumed with terrors.
As a dream when one awaketh; so, O Lord, when thou awakest,
thou shalt despise their image.
Thus my heart was grieved, and I was pricked in my reins.
So foolish was I, and ignorant: I was as a beast before thee.
Nevertheless I am continually with thee: thou hast holden me
by my right hand.
Thou shalt guide me with thy counsel, and afterward receive me
to glory.
Whom have I in heaven but thee? and there is none upon earth
that I desire besides thee.
My flesh and my heart faileth: but God is the strength of my
heart, and my portion forever.
For, lo, they that are far from thee shall perish: thou hast
destroyed all them that go a whoring from thee.
But it is good for me to draw near to God: I have put my trust in
the Lord God, that I may declare all thy works.

*This is the first psalm of Book 3. Feet, eyes, mouth,
and heart are mentioned in the first nine verses.
Step, see, speak, and sense this prayer.*

Psalm 74

O God, why hast thou cast us off forever? why doth thine anger
  smoke against the sheep of thy pasture?
Remember thy congregation, which thou hast purchased of old;
  the rod of thine inheritance, which thou hast redeemed;
  this mount Zion, wherein thou hast dwelt.
Lift up thy feet unto the perpetual desolations; even all that the
  enemy hath done wickedly in the sanctuary.
Thine enemies roar in the midst of thy congregations; they set
  up their ensigns for signs.
A man was famous according as he had lifted up axes upon the
  thick trees.
But now they break down the carved work thereof at once with
  axes and hammers.
They have cast fire into thy sanctuary, they have defiled by
  casting down the dwelling place of thy name to the ground.
They said in their hearts, Let us destroy them together: they
  have burned up all the synagogues of God in the land.
We see not our signs: there is no more any prophet: neither is
  there among us any that knoweth how long.
O God, how long shall the adversary reproach? shall the enemy
  blaspheme thy name forever?
Why withdrawest thou thy hand, even thy right hand? pluck it
  out of thy bosom.
For God is my King of old, working salvation in the midst of
  the earth.
Thou didst divide the sea by thy strength: thou brakest the
  heads of the dragons in the waters.
Thou brakest the heads of leviathan in pieces, and gavest him to
  be meat to the people inhabiting the wilderness.
Thou didst cleave the fountain and the flood: thou driedst up
  mighty rivers.
The day is thine, the night also is thine: thou hast prepared the
  light and the sun.

Thou hast set all the borders of the earth: thou hast made
summer and winter.

Remember this, that the enemy hath reproached, O Lord, and
that the foolish people have blasphemed thy name.

O deliver not the soul of thy turtledove unto the multitude
of the wicked: forget not the congregation of thy poor
forever.

Have respect unto the covenant: for the dark places of the earth
are full of the habitations of cruelty.

O let not the oppressed return ashamed: let the poor and needy
praise thy name.

Arise, O God, plead thine own cause: remember how the
foolish man reproacheth thee daily.

Forget not the voice of thine enemies: the tumult of those that
rise up against thee increaseth continually.

---

*Are you surprised by the mention of dragons
and a leviathan in the Bible? What do you think it means?*

Psalm 75

Unto thee, O God, do we give thanks, unto thee do we give thanks: for that thy name is near thy wondrous works declare.

When I shall receive the congregation I will judge uprightly.

The earth and all the inhabitants thereof are dissolved: I bear up the pillars of it. Selah.

I said unto the fools, Deal not foolishly: and to the wicked, Lift not up the horn:

Lift not up your horn on high: speak not with a stiff neck.

For promotion cometh neither from the east, nor from the west, nor from the south.

But God is the judge: he putteth down one, and setteth up another.

For in the hand of the Lord there is a cup, and the wine is red; it is full of mixture; and he poureth out of the same: but the dregs thereof, all the wicked of the earth shall wring them out, and drink them.

But I will declare forever; I will sing praises to the God of Jacob.

All the horns of the wicked also will I cut off; but the horns of the righteous shall be exalted.

What does the word "horn," which is mentioned four times, symbolize?

ᴾsalm 76

In Judah is God known: his name is great in Israel.

In Salem also is his tabernacle, and his dwelling place in Zion.

There brake he the arrows of the bow, the shield, and the sword, and the battle. Selah.

Thou art more glorious and excellent than the mountains of prey.

The stout-hearted are spoiled, they have slept their sleep: and none of the men of might have found their hands.

At thy rebuke, O God of Jacob, both the chariot and horse are cast into a dead sleep.

Thou, even thou, art to be feared: and who may stand in thy sight when once thou art angry?

Thou didst cause judgment to be heard from heaven; the earth feared, and was still,

When God arose to judgment, to save all the meek of the earth. Selah.

Surely the wrath of man shall praise thee: the remainder of wrath shalt thou restrain.

Vow, and pay unto the Lord your God: let all that be round about him bring presents unto him that ought to be feared.

He shall cut off the spirit of princes: he is terrible to the kings of the earth.

What do you think the circumstances were
when this psalm was written?

Psalm 77

I cried unto God with my voice, even unto God with my voice;
    and he gave ear unto me.

In the day of my trouble I sought the Lord: my sore ran in the
    night, and ceased not: my soul refused to be comforted.

I remembered God, and was troubled: I complained, and my
    spirit was overwhelmed. Selah.

Thou holdest mine eyes waking: I am so troubled that I cannot
    speak.

I have considered the days of old, the years of ancient times.

I call to remembrance my song in the night: I commune with
    mine own heart: and my spirit made diligent search.

Will the Lord cast off forever? and will he be favorable no
    more?

Is his mercy clean gone forever? doth his promise fail
    forevermore?

Hath God forgotten to be gracious? hath he in anger shut up
    his tender mercies? Selah.

And I said, This is my infirmity: but I will remember the years of
    the right hand of the Most High.

I will remember the works of the Lord: surely I will remember
    thy wonders of old.

I will meditate also of all thy work, and talk of thy doings.

Thy way, O God, is in the sanctuary: who is so great a God as
    our God?

Thou art the God that doest wonders: thou hast declared thy
    strength among the people.

Thou hast with thine arm redeemed thy people, the sons of
    Jacob and Joseph. Selah.

The waters saw thee, O God, the waters saw thee; they were
    afraid: the depths also were troubled.

The clouds poured out water: the skies sent out a sound: thine
    arrows also went abroad.

The voice of thy thunder was in the heaven: the lightnings lightened the world: the earth trembled and shook.

Thy way is in the sea, and thy path in the great waters, and thy footsteps are not known.

Thou leddest thy people like a flock by the hand of Moses and Aaron.

Reflect on how nature seems to be a witness to God.

Psalm 78

Give ear, O my people, to my law: incline your ears to the
   words of my mouth.

I will open my mouth in a parable: I will utter dark sayings of
   old:

Which we have heard and known, and our fathers have told us.

We will not hide them from their children, showing to the
   generation to come the praises of the Lord, and his
   strength, and his wonderful works that he hath done.

For he established a testimony in Jacob, and appointed a law in
   Israel, which he commanded our fathers, that they should
   make them known to their children:

That the generation to come might know them, even the
   children which should be born; who should arise and
   declare them to their children:

That they might set their hope in God, and not forget the
   works of God, but keep his commandments:

And might not be as their fathers, a stubborn and rebellious
   generation; a generation that set not their heart aright, and
   whose spirit was not steadfast with God.

The children of Ephraim, being armed, and carrying bows,
   turned back in the day of battle.

They kept not the covenant of God, and refused to walk in his
   law;

And forgat his works, and his wonders that he had showed
   them.

Marvelous things did he in the sight of their fathers, in the land
   of Egypt, in the field of Zoan.

He divided the sea, and caused them to pass through; and he
   made the waters to stand as a heap.

In the daytime also he led them with a cloud, and all the night
   with a light of fire.

He clave the rocks in the wilderness, and gave them drink as
   out of the great depths.

He brought streams also out of the rock, and caused waters to
    run down like rivers.

And they sinned yet more against him by provoking the Most
    High in the wilderness.

And they tempted God in their heart by asking meat for their
    lust.

Yea, they spake against God; they said, Can God furnish a table
    in the wilderness?

Behold, he smote the rock, that the waters gushed out, and the
    streams overflowed; can he give bread also? can he provide
    flesh for his people?

Therefore the Lord heard this, and was wroth: so a fire was
    kindled against Jacob, and anger also came up against Israel;

Because they believed not in God, and trusted not in his
    salvation:

Though he had commanded the clouds from above, and opened
    the doors of heaven,

And had rained down manna upon them to eat, and had given
    them of the corn of heaven.

Man did eat angels' food: he sent them meat to the full.

He caused an east wind to blow in the heaven: and by his
    power he brought in the south wind.

He rained flesh also upon them as dust, and feathered fowls like
    as the sand of the sea:

And he let it fall in the midst of their camp, round about their
    habitations.

So they did eat, and were well filled: for he gave them their own
    desire;

They were not estranged from their lust: but while their meat
    was yet in their mouths,

The wrath of God came upon them, and slew the fattest of
    them, and smote down the chosen men of Israel.

For all this they sinned still, and believed not for his wondrous
    works.

Therefore their days did he consume in vanity, and their years in trouble.

When he slew them, then they sought him: and they returned and inquired early after God.

And they remembered that God was their rock, and the high God their redeemer.

Nevertheless they did flatter him with their mouth, and they lied unto him with their tongues.

For their heart was not right with him, neither were they steadfast in his covenant.

But he, being full of compassion, forgave their iniquity, and destroyed them not: yea, many a time turned he his anger away, and did not stir up all his wrath.

For he remembered that they were but flesh; a wind that passeth away, and cometh not again.

How oft did they provoke him in the wilderness, and grieve him in the desert!

Yea, they turned back and tempted God, and limited the Holy One of Israel.

They remembered not his hand, nor the day when he delivered them from the enemy:

How he had wrought his signs in Egypt, and his wonders in the field of Zoan:

And had turned their rivers into blood; and their floods, that they could not drink.

He sent divers sorts of flies among them, which devoured them; and frogs, which destroyed them.

He gave also their increase unto the caterpillar, and their labor unto the locust.

He destroyed their vines with hail, and their sycamore trees with frost.

He gave up their cattle also to the hail, and their flocks to hot thunderbolts.

He cast upon them the fierceness of his anger, wrath, and
    indignation, and trouble, by sending evil angels among
    them.
He made a way to his anger; he spared not their soul from
    death, but gave their life over to the pestilence;
And smote all the firstborn in Egypt; the chief of their strength
    in the tabernacles of Ham:
But made his own people to go forth like sheep, and guided
    them in the wilderness like a flock.
And he led them on safely, so that they feared not: but the sea
    overwhelmed their enemies.
And he brought them to the border of his sanctuary, even to
    this mountain, which his right hand had purchased.
He cast out the heathen also before them, and divided them an
    inheritance by line, and made the tribes of Israel to dwell in
    their tents.
Yet they tempted and provoked the most high God, and kept
    not his testimonies:
But turned back, and dealt unfaithfully like their fathers: they
    were turned aside like a deceitful bow.
For they provoked him to anger with their high places, and
    moved him to jealousy with their graven images.
When God heard this, he was wroth, and greatly abhorred Israel:
So that he forsook the tabernacle of Shiloh, the tent which he
    placed among men;
And delivered his strength into captivity, and his glory into the
    enemy's hand.
He gave his people over also unto the sword; and was wroth
    with his inheritance.
The fire consumed their young men; and their maidens were not
    given to marriage.
Their priests fell by the sword; and their widows made no
    lamentation.

Then the Lord awaked as one out of sleep, and like a mighty
man that shouteth by reason of wine.
And he smote his enemies in the hinder parts: he put them to a
perpetual reproach.
Moreover he refused the tabernacle of Joseph, and chose not
the tribe of Ephraim:
But chose the tribe of Judah, the mount Zion which he loved.
And he built his sanctuary like high palaces, like the earth
which he hath established forever.
He chose David also his servant, and took him from the
sheepfolds:
From following the ewes great with young he brought him to
feed Jacob his people, and Israel his inheritance.
So he fed them according to the integrity of his heart; and
guided them by the skilfulness of his hands.

Can you envision this psalm as a graphic novel or comic book?
Would the message reach more people in that format?

Psalm 79

O God, the heathen are come into thine inheritance; thy holy
    temple have they defiled; they have laid Jerusalem on
    heaps.

The dead bodies of thy servants have they given to be meat
    unto the fowls of the heaven, the flesh of thy saints unto
    the beasts of the earth.

Their blood have they shed like water round about Jerusalem;
    and there was none to bury them.

We are become a reproach to our neighbors, a scorn and
    derision to them that are round about us.

How long, Lord? wilt thou be angry forever? shall thy jealousy
    burn like fire?

Pour out thy wrath upon the heathen that have not known
    thee, and upon the kingdoms that have not called upon thy
    name.

For they have devoured Jacob, and laid waste his dwelling
    place.

O remember not against us former iniquities: let thy tender
    mercies speedily prevent us; for we are brought very low.

Help us, O God of our salvation, for the glory of thy name: and
    deliver us, and purge away our sins, for thy name's sake.
Wherefore should the heathen say, Where is their God? let him
    be known among the heathen in our sight by the revenging
    of the blood of thy servants which is shed.
Let the sighing of the prisoner come before thee; according
    to the greatness of thy power preserve thou those that are
    appointed to die;
And render unto our neighbors sevenfold into their bosom their
    reproach, wherewith they have reproached thee, O Lord.
So we thy people and sheep of thy pasture will give thee thanks
    forever: we will show forth thy praise to all generations.

Who do you say are "the heathens"?
Who do you say are God's people?

ʻPsalm 80

Give ear, O Shepherd of Israel, thou that leadest Joseph like a
  flock; thou that dwellest between the cherubim, shine forth.

Before Ephraim and Benjamin and Manasseh stir up thy
  strength, and come and save us.

Turn us again, O God, and cause thy face to shine; and we shall
  be saved.

O Lord God of hosts, how long wilt thou be angry against the
  prayer of thy people?

Thou feedest them with the bread of tears; and givest them
  tears to drink in great measure.

Thou makest us a strife unto our neighbors: and our enemies
  laugh among themselves.

Turn us again, O God of hosts, and cause thy face to shine; and
  we shall be saved.

Thou hast brought a vine out of Egypt: thou hast cast out the
  heathen, and planted it.

Thou preparedst room before it, and didst cause it to take deep
  root, and it filled the land.

The hills were covered with the shadow of it, and the boughs
  thereof were like the goodly cedars.

She sent out her boughs unto the sea, and her branches unto
  the river.

Why hast thou then broken down her hedges, so that all they
  which pass by the way do pluck her?

The boar out of the wood doth waste it, and the wild beast of
  the field doth devour it.

Return, we beseech thee, O God of hosts: look down from
  heaven, and behold, and visit this vine;

And the vineyard which thy right hand hath planted, and the
  branch that thou madest strong for thyself.

It is burned with fire, it is cut down: they perish at the rebuke of
  thy countenance.

Let thy hand be upon the man of thy right hand, upon the son
of man whom thou madest strong for thyself.
So will not we go back from thee: quicken us, and we will call
upon thy name.
Turn us again, O Lord God of hosts, cause thy face to shine;
and we shall be saved.

---

*The phrase "Turn us again, O Lord God of hosts, and cause thy face
to shine; and we shall be saved," appears three times in this psalm.
Can you imagine this as a song?*

Psalm 81

Sing aloud unto God our strength: make a joyful noise unto the
God of Jacob.

Take a psalm, and bring hither the timbrel, the pleasant harp
with the psaltery.

Blow up the trumpet in the new moon, in the time appointed,
on our solemn feast day.

For this was a statute for Israel, and a law of the God of Jacob.

This he ordained in Joseph for a testimony, when he went out
through the land of Egypt: where I heard a language that I
understood not.

I removed his shoulder from the burden: his hands were
delivered from the pots.

Thou calledst in trouble, and I delivered thee; I answered thee
in the secret place of thunder: I proved thee at the waters of
Meribah. Selah.

Hear, O my people, and I will testify unto thee: O Israel, if thou
wilt hearken unto me;

There shall no strange god be in thee; neither shalt thou
worship any strange god.

I am the Lord thy God, which brought thee out of the land of
Egypt: open thy mouth wide, and I will fill it.

But my people would not hearken to my voice; and Israel would
none of me.

So I gave them up unto their own hearts' lust: and they walked
in their own counsels.

Oh that my people had hearkened unto me, and Israel had
walked in my ways!

I should soon have subdued their enemies, and turned my hand
against their adversaries.

The haters of the Lord should have submitted themselves unto him: but their time should have endured forever.
He should have fed them also with the finest of the wheat: and with honey out of the rock should I have satisfied thee.

Some theologians have called this psalm "the poetic center of the Psalter" because it is Book 3 of 5 and is the middle psalm (8 of 17). What significance, if any, is there to this?

Psalm 82

God standeth in the congregation of the mighty; he judgeth among the gods.

How long will ye judge unjustly, and accept the persons of the wicked? Selah.

Defend the poor and fatherless: do justice to the afflicted and needy.

Deliver the poor and needy: rid them out of the hand of the wicked.

They know not, neither will they understand; they walk on in darkness: all the foundations of the earth are out of course.

I have said, Ye are gods; and all of you are children of the Most High.

But ye shall die like men, and fall like one of the princes.

Arise, O God, judge the earth: for thou shalt inherit all nations.

How will you heed the call to social justice?

Psalm 83

Keep not thou silence, O God: hold not thy peace, and be not
still, O God.

For, lo, thine enemies make a tumult: and they that hate thee
have lifted up the head.

They have taken crafty counsel against thy people, and
consulted against thy hidden ones.

They have said, Come, and let us cut them off from being
a nation; that the name of Israel may be no more in
remembrance.

For they have consulted together with one consent: they are
confederate against thee:

The tabernacles of Edom, and the Ishmaelites; of Moab, and the
Hagarenes;

Gebal, and Ammon, and Amalek; the Philistines with the
inhabitants of Tyre;

Assur also is joined with them: they have helped the children of
Lot. Selah.

Do unto them as unto the Midianites; as to Sisera, as to Jabin, at
the brook of Kison:

Which perished at Endor: they became as dung for the earth.

Make their nobles like Oreb, and like Zeeb: yea, all their
princes as Zebah, and as Zalmunna:

Who said, Let us take to ourselves the houses of God in
possession.

O my God, make them like a wheel; as the stubble before the
wind.

As the fire burneth a wood, and as the flame setteth the
mountains on fire;

So persecute them with thy tempest, and make them afraid with
thy storm.

Fill their faces with shame; that they may seek thy name,
O Lord.

Let them be confounded and troubled forever; yea, let them be put to shame, and perish:

That men may know that thou, whose name alone is Jehovah, art the Most High over all the earth.

———

What people or things keep you from God?

Psalm 84

How amiable are thy tabernacles, O Lord of hosts!

My soul longeth, yea, even fainteth for the courts of the Lord:
my heart and my flesh crieth out for the living God.

Yea, the sparrow hath found a house, and the swallow a nest for
herself, where she may lay her young, even thine altars,
O Lord of hosts, my King, and my God.

Blessed are they that dwell in thy house: they will be still
praising thee. Selah.

Blessed is the man whose strength is in thee; in whose heart are
the ways of them.

Who passing through the valley of Baca make it a well; the rain
also filleth the pools.

They go from strength to strength, every one of them in Zion
appeareth before God.

O Lord God of hosts, hear my prayer: give ear, O God of Jacob.
Selah.

Behold, O God our shield, and look upon the face of thine anointed.

For a day in thy courts is better than a thousand. I had rather be
a doorkeeper in the house of my God, than to dwell in the
tents of wickedness.

For the Lord God is a sun and shield: the Lord will give grace
and glory: no good thing will he withhold from them that
walk uprightly.

O Lord of hosts, blessed is the man that trusteth in thee.

What are the three beatitudes in this psalm?

Psalm 85

Lord, thou hast been favorable unto thy land: thou hast brought back the captivity of Jacob.

Thou hast forgiven the iniquity of thy people; thou hast covered all their sin. Selah.

Thou hast taken away all thy wrath: thou hast turned thyself from the fierceness of thine anger.

Turn us, O God of our salvation, and cause thine anger toward us to cease.

Wilt thou be angry with us forever? wilt thou draw out thine anger to all generations?

Wilt thou not revive us again: that thy people may rejoice in thee?

Show us thy mercy, O Lord, and grant us thy salvation.

I will hear what God the Lord will speak: for he will speak peace unto his people, and to his saints: but let them not turn again to folly.

Surely his salvation is nigh them that fear him; that glory may dwell in our land.

Mercy and truth are met together; righteousness and peace have kissed each other.

Truth shall spring out of the earth; and righteousness shall look down from heaven.

Yea, the Lord shall give that which is good; and our land shall
    yield her increase.
Righteousness shall go before him; and shall set us in the way of
    his steps.

*Contemplate the four virtues: Mercy and Truth, Righteousness
(Justice) and Peace. How are these evident in your life?*

Psalm 86

Bow down thine ear, O Lord, hear me: for I am poor and needy.

Preserve my soul; for I am holy: O thou my God, save thy
servant that trusteth in thee.

Be merciful unto me, O Lord: for I cry unto thee daily.

Rejoice the soul of thy servant: for unto thee, O Lord, do I lift
up my soul.

For thou, Lord, art good, and ready to forgive; and plenteous in
mercy unto all them that call upon thee.

Give ear, O Lord, unto my prayer; and attend to the voice of
my supplications.

In the day of my trouble I will call upon thee: for thou wilt
answer me.

Among the gods there is none like unto thee, O Lord; neither
are there any works like unto thy works.

All nations whom thou hast made shall come and worship
before thee, O Lord; and shall glorify thy name.

For thou art great, and doest wondrous things: thou art God
alone.

Teach me thy way, O Lord; I will walk in thy truth: unite my
heart to fear thy name.

I will praise thee, O Lord my God, with all my heart: and I will
glorify thy name forevermore.

For great is thy mercy toward me: and thou hast delivered my
soul from the lowest hell.

O God, the proud are risen against me, and the assemblies of
violent men have sought after my soul; and have not set
thee before them.

But thou, O Lord, art a God full of compassion, and gracious,
long-suffering, and plenteous in mercy and truth.

O turn unto me, and have mercy upon me; give thy strength
unto thy servant, and save the son of thine handmaid.

Show me a token for good; that they which hate me may see it, and be ashamed: because thou, Lord, hast helped me, and comforted me.

———————

Find different hymns based on this psalm and listen to them. Does one of them speak to you more than the others? Why?

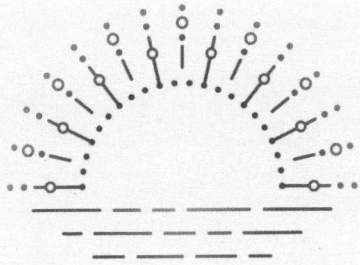

Psalm 87

His foundation is in the holy mountains.

The Lord loveth the gates of Zion more than all the dwellings
of Jacob.

Glorious things are spoken of thee, O city of God. Selah.

I will make mention of Rahab and Babylon to them that know
me: behold Philistia, and Tyre, with Ethiopia; this man was
born there.

And of Zion it shall be said, This and that man was born in her:
and the Highest himself shall establish her.

The Lord shall count, when he writeth up the people, that this
man was born there. Selah.

As well the singers as the players on instruments shall be there:
all my springs are in thee.

Everyone strives for or dreams of the city of God.
Where does this place exist now in this world?

Psalm 88

O Lord God of my salvation, I have cried day and night before
thee:

Let my prayer come before thee: incline thine ear unto my cry;

For my soul is full of troubles: and my life draweth nigh unto
the grave.

I am counted with them that go down into the pit: I am as a
man that hath no strength:

Free among the dead, like the slain that lie in the grave, whom
thou rememberest no more: and they are cut off from thy
hand.

Thou hast laid me in the lowest pit, in darkness, in the deeps.

Thy wrath lieth hard upon me, and thou hast afflicted me with
all thy waves. Selah.

Thou hast put away mine acquaintance far from me; thou hast
made me an abomination unto them: I am shut up, and I
cannot come forth.

Mine eye mourneth by reason of affliction: Lord, I have called
daily upon thee, I have stretched out my hands unto thee.

Wilt thou show wonders to the dead? shall the dead arise and
praise thee? Selah.

Shall thy loving-kindness be declared in the grave? or thy
faithfulness in destruction?

Shall thy wonders be known in the dark? and thy righteousness
in the land of forgetfulness?

But unto thee have I cried, O Lord; and in the morning shall my
prayer prevent thee.

Lord, why castest thou off my soul? why hidest thou thy face
from me?

I am afflicted and ready to die from my youth up: while I suffer
thy terrors I am distracted.

Thy fierce wrath goeth over me; thy terrors have cut me off.

They came round about me daily like water; they compassed
me about together.
Lover and friend hast thou put far from me, and mine
acquaintance into darkness.

When did you experience "the lowest pit, in darkness, in the deeps"?
How did you get out of that place?

Psalm 89

I will sing of the mercies of the Lord forever: with my mouth
will I make known thy faithfulness to all generations.

For I have said, Mercy shall be built up forever: thy faithfulness
shalt thou establish in the very heavens.

I have made a covenant with my chosen, I have sworn unto
David my servant,

Thy seed will I establish forever, and build up thy throne to all
generations. Selah.

And the heavens shall praise thy wonders, O Lord: thy
faithfulness also in the congregation of the saints.

For who in the heaven can be compared unto the Lord? who
among the sons of the mighty can be likened unto the
Lord?

God is greatly to be feared in the assembly of the saints, and to
be had in reverence of all them that are about him.

O Lord God of hosts, who is a strong Lord like unto thee? or to
thy faithfulness round about thee?

Thou rulest the raging of the sea: when the waves thereof arise,
thou stillest them.

Thou hast broken Rahab in pieces, as one that is slain; thou hast
scattered thine enemies with thy strong arm.

The heavens are thine, the earth also is thine: as for the world
and the fulness thereof, thou hast founded them.

The north and the south thou hast created them: Tabor and
Hermon shall rejoice in thy name.

Thou hast a mighty arm: strong is thy hand, and high is thy
right hand.

Justice and judgment are the habitation of thy throne: mercy
and truth shall go before thy face.

Blessed is the people that know the joyful sound: they shall
walk, O Lord, in the light of thy countenance.

In thy name shall they rejoice all the day: and in thy
righteousness shall they be exalted.

For thou art the glory of their strength: and in thy favor our
horn shall be exalted.

For the Lord is our defense; and the Holy One of Israel is our
King.

Then thou spakest in vision to thy holy one, and saidst, I have
laid help upon one that is mighty; I have exalted one
chosen out of the people.

I have found David my servant; with my holy oil have I
anointed him:

With whom my hand shall be established: mine arm also shall
strengthen him.

The enemy shall not exact upon him; nor the son of wickedness
afflict him.

And I will beat down his foes before his face, and plague them
that hate him.

But my faithfulness and my mercy shall be with him: and in my
name shall his horn be exalted.

I will set his hand also in the sea, and his right hand in the
rivers.

He shall cry unto me, Thou art my father, my God, and the
rock of my salvation.

Also I will make him my firstborn, higher than the kings of the
earth.

My mercy will I keep for him forevermore, and my covenant
shall stand fast with him.

His seed also will I make to endure forever, and his throne as
the days of heaven.

If his children forsake my law, and walk not in my judgments;

If they break my statutes, and keep not my commandments;

Then will I visit their transgression with the rod, and their
iniquity with stripes.

Nevertheless my loving-kindness will I not utterly take from him, nor suffer my faithfulness to fail.

My covenant will I not break, nor alter the thing that is gone out of my lips.

Once have I sworn by my holiness that I will not lie unto David.

His seed shall endure forever, and his throne as the sun before me.

It shall be established forever as the moon, and as a faithful witness in heaven. Selah.

But thou hast cast off and abhorred, thou hast been wroth with thine anointed.

Thou hast made void the covenant of thy servant: thou hast profaned his crown by casting it to the ground.

Thou hast broken down all his hedges; thou hast brought his strongholds to ruin.

All that pass by the way spoil him: he is a reproach to his neighbors.

Thou hast set up the right hand of his adversaries; thou hast made all his enemies to rejoice.

Thou hast also turned the edge of his sword, and hast not made him to stand in the battle.

Thou hast made his glory to cease, and cast his throne down to the ground.

The days of his youth hast thou shortened: thou hast covered him with shame. Selah.

How long, Lord? wilt thou hide thyself forever? shall thy wrath burn like fire?

Remember how short my time is: wherefore hast thou made all men in vain?

What man is he that liveth, and shall not see death? shall he deliver his soul from the hand of the grave? Selah.

Lord, where are thy former loving-kindnesses, which thou swarest unto David in thy truth?

Remember, Lord, the reproach of thy servants; how I do bear in
    my bosom the reproach of all the mighty people;
Wherewith thine enemies have reproached, O Lord; wherewith
    they have reproached the footsteps of thine anointed.
Blessed be the Lord forevermore. Amen, and Amen.

This is the final psalm of Book 3 of 5.
What do you take away from it?

Psalm 90

Lord, thou hast been our dwelling place in all generations.

Before the mountains were brought forth, or ever thou hadst formed the earth and the world, even from everlasting to everlasting, thou art God.

Thou turnest man to destruction; and sayest, Return, ye children of men.

For a thousand years in thy sight are but as yesterday when it is past, and as a watch in the night.

Thou carriest them away as with a flood; they are as a sleep: in the morning they are like grass which groweth up.

In the morning it flourisheth, and groweth up; in the evening it is cut down, and withereth.

For we are consumed by thine anger, and by thy wrath are we troubled.

Thou hast set our iniquities before thee, our secret sins in the light of thy countenance.

For all our days are passed away in thy wrath: we spend our years as a tale that is told.

The days of our years are threescore years and ten; and if by reason of strength they be fourscore years, yet is their strength labor and sorrow; for it is soon cut off, and we fly away.

Who knoweth the power of thine anger? even according to thy fear, so is thy wrath.

So teach us to number our days, that we may apply our hearts unto wisdom.

Return, O Lord, how long? and let it repent thee concerning thy servants.

O satisfy us early with thy mercy; that we may rejoice and be glad all our days.

Make us glad according to the days wherein thou hast afflicted us, and the years wherein we have seen evil.

Let thy work appear unto thy servants, and thy glory unto their
children.
And let the beauty of the Lord our God be upon us: and
establish thou the work of our hands upon us; yea, the work
of our hands establish thou it.

This first psalm of Book 4 spurs us to think about how we shall
live our life, "for it is soon cut off, and we fly away."
How do you "spend [your] years as a tale that is told"?

Psalm 91

He that dwelleth in the secret place of the Most High shall abide under the shadow of the Almighty.

I will say of the Lord, He is my refuge and my fortress: my God; in him will I trust.

Surely he shall deliver thee from the snare of the fowler, and from the noisome pestilence.

He shall cover thee with his feathers, and under his wings shalt thou trust: his truth shall be thy shield and buckler.

Thou shalt not be afraid for the terror by night; nor for the arrow that flieth by day;

Nor for the pestilence that walketh in darkness; nor for the destruction that wasteth at noonday.

A thousand shall fall at thy side, and ten thousand at thy right hand; but it shall not come nigh thee.

Only with thine eyes shalt thou behold and see the reward of the wicked.

Because thou hast made the Lord, which is my refuge, even the Most High, thy habitation;

There shall no evil befall thee, neither shall any plague come nigh thy dwelling.

For he shall give his angels charge over thee, to keep thee in all thy ways.

They shall bear thee up in their hands, lest thou dash thy foot against a stone.

Thou shalt tread upon the lion and adder: the young lion and the dragon shalt thou trample under feet.

Because he hath set his love upon me, therefore will I deliver him: I will set him on high, because he hath known my name.

He shall call upon me, and I will answer him: I will be with him
   in trouble; I will deliver him, and honor him.
With long life will I satisfy him, and show him my salvation.

What is your favorite image in this psalm?

Psalm 92

It is a good thing to give thanks unto the Lord, and to sing
  praises unto thy name, O Most High:
To show forth thy loving-kindness in the morning, and thy
  faithfulness every night,
Upon an instrument of ten strings, and upon the psaltery; upon
  the harp with a solemn sound.
For thou, Lord, hast made me glad through thy work: I will
  triumph in the works of thy hands.
O Lord, how great are thy works! and thy thoughts are very deep.
A brutish man knoweth not; neither doth a fool understand this.
When the wicked spring as the grass, and when all the workers of
  iniquity do flourish; it is that they shall be destroyed forever:
But thou, Lord, art most high forevermore.
For, lo, thine enemies, O Lord, for, lo, thine enemies shall
  perish; all the workers of iniquity shall be scattered.
But my horn shalt thou exalt like the horn of a unicorn: I shall
  be anointed with fresh oil.
Mine eye also shall see my desire on mine enemies, and mine ears
  shall hear my desire of the wicked that rise up against me.
The righteous shall flourish like the palm tree: he shall grow like
  a cedar in Lebanon.
Those that be planted in the house of the Lord shall flourish in
  the courts of our God.
They shall still bring forth fruit in old age; they shall be fat and
  flourishing;
To show that the Lord is upright: he is my rock, and there is no
  unrighteousness in him.

Recite this psalm at the beginning of your sabbath,
as some theologians and Jewish scholars speculate
Adam did in the Garden of Eden.

Psalm 93

The Lord reigneth, he is clothed with majesty; the Lord is
    clothed with strength, wherewith he hath girded himself:
    the world also is stablished, that it cannot be moved.
Thy throne is established of old: thou art from everlasting.
The floods have lifted up, O Lord, the floods have lifted up
    their voice; the floods lift up their waves.
The Lord on high is mightier than the noise of many waters,
    yea, than the mighty waves of the sea.
Thy testimonies are very sure: holiness becometh thine house,
    O Lord, forever.

*Find the different hymns that are inspired by this short psalm,
including CeCe Winans's performance of "Holiness Becometh
Thine House O Lord." How do these songs make you feel?*

Psalm 94

O Lord God, to whom vengeance belongeth; O God, to whom
vengeance belongeth, show thyself.

Lift up thyself, thou judge of the earth: render a reward to the
proud.

Lord, how long shall the wicked, how long shall the wicked
triumph?

How long shall they utter and speak hard things? and all the
workers of iniquity boast themselves?

They break in pieces thy people, O Lord, and afflict thine
heritage.

They slay the widow and the stranger, and murder the
fatherless.

Yet they say, The Lord shall not see, neither shall the God of
Jacob regard it.

Understand, ye brutish among the people: and ye fools, when
will ye be wise?

He that planted the ear, shall he not hear? he that formed the
eye, shall he not see?

He that chastiseth the heathen, shall not he correct? he that
teacheth man knowledge, shall not he know?

The Lord knoweth the thoughts of man, that they are vanity.

Blessed is the man whom thou chastenest, O Lord, and teachest
him out of thy law;

That thou mayest give him rest from the days of adversity, until
the pit be digged for the wicked.

For the Lord will not cast off his people, neither will he forsake
his inheritance.

But judgment shall return unto righteousness: and all the
upright in heart shall follow it.

Who will rise up for me against the evildoers? or who will stand
up for me against the workers of iniquity?

Unless the Lord had been my help, my soul had almost dwelt in
silence.

When I said, My foot slippeth; thy mercy, O Lord, held me up.

In the multitude of my thoughts within me thy comforts delight my soul.

Shall the throne of iniquity have fellowship with thee, which frameth mischief by a law?

They gather themselves together against the soul of the righteous, and condemn the innocent blood.

But the Lord is my defense; and my God is the rock of my refuge.

And he shall bring upon them their own iniquity, and shall cut them off in their own wickedness; yea, the Lord our God shall cut them off.

How does it feel that you can call on God to smite "the evildoers"?

Psalm 95

O come, let us sing unto the Lord: let us make a joyful noise to the rock of our salvation.

Let us come before his presence with thanksgiving, and make a joyful noise unto him with psalms.

For the Lord is a great God, and a great King above all gods.

In his hand are the deep places of the earth: the strength of the hills is his also.

The sea is his, and he made it: and his hands formed the dry land.

O come, let us worship and bow down: let us kneel before the Lord our maker.

For he is our God; and we are the people of his pasture, and the sheep of his hand. To-day if ye will hear his voice,

Harden not your heart, as in the provocation, and as in the day of temptation in the wilderness:

When your fathers tempted me, proved me, and saw my work.

Forty years long was I grieved with this generation, and said, It is a people that do err in their heart, and they have not known my ways:

Unto whom I sware in my wrath that they should not enter into my rest.

What does your joyful noise sound like? Celebrate that today.

Psalm 96

O sing unto the Lord a new song: sing unto the Lord, all the earth.

Sing unto the Lord, bless his name; show forth his salvation from day to day.

Declare his glory among the heathen, his wonders among all people.

For the Lord is great, and greatly to be praised: he is to be feared above all gods.

For all the gods of the nations are idols: but the Lord made the heavens.

Honor and majesty are before him: strength and beauty are in his sanctuary.

Give unto the Lord, O ye kindreds of the people, give unto the Lord glory and strength.

Give unto the Lord the glory due unto his name: bring an offering, and come into his courts.

O worship the Lord in the beauty of holiness: fear before him, all the earth.

Say among the heathen that the Lord reigneth: the world also shall be established that it shall not be moved: he shall judge the people righteously.

Let the heavens rejoice, and let the earth be glad; let the sea roar, and the fulness thereof.

Let the field be joyful, and all that is therein: then shall all the trees of the wood rejoice

Before the Lord: for he cometh, for he cometh to judge the earth: he shall judge the world with righteousness, and the people with his truth.

The word "sing" is used three times in this psalm, which pertains to morning, noon, and evening prayers in Judaism. Consider singing your prayers today.

Psalm 97

The Lord reigneth; let the earth rejoice; let the multitude of
    isles be glad thereof.

Clouds and darkness are round about him: righteousness and
    judgment are the habitation of his throne.

A fire goeth before him, and burneth up his enemies round about.

His lightnings enlightened the world: the earth saw, and trembled.

The hills melted like wax at the presence of the Lord, at the
    presence of the Lord of the whole earth.

The heavens declare his righteousness, and all the people see
    his glory.

Confounded be all they that serve graven images, that boast
    themselves of idols: worship him, all ye gods.

Zion heard, and was glad; and the daughters of Judah rejoiced
    because of thy judgments, O Lord.

For thou, Lord, art high above all the earth: thou art exalted far
    above all gods.

Ye that love the Lord, hate evil: he preserveth the souls of his
    saints; he delivereth them out of the hand of the wicked.

Light is sown for the righteous, and gladness for the upright in heart.

Rejoice in the Lord, ye righteous; and give thanks at the
    remembrance of his holiness.

What appeals to you about this psalm?

ꞌPsalm 98

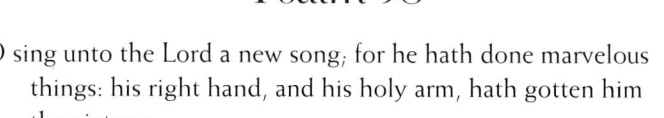

O sing unto the Lord a new song; for he hath done marvelous
 things: his right hand, and his holy arm, hath gotten him
 the victory.
The Lord hath made known his salvation: his righteousness
 hath he openly showed in the sight of the heathen.
He hath remembered his mercy and his truth toward the house
 of Israel: all the ends of the earth have seen the salvation of
 our God.
Make a joyful noise unto the Lord, all the earth: make a loud
 noise, and rejoice, and sing praise.
Sing unto the Lord with the harp; with the harp, and the voice
 of a psalm.
With trumpets and sound of cornet make a joyful noise before
 the Lord, the King.
Let the sea roar, and the fulness thereof; the world, and they
 that dwell therein.
Let the floods clap their hands: let the hills be joyful together
Before the Lord; for he cometh to judge the earth: with
 righteousness shall he judge the world, and the people with
 equity.

*Isaac Watts, poet and clergyman, drew inspiration from verses 4—9
of this psalm to write the lyrics to the Christmas carol "Joy to the
World." Listen to the song and see if it brings joy to your day.*

Psalm 99

The Lord reigneth; let the people tremble: he sitteth between the cherubim; let the earth be moved.

The Lord is great in Zion; and he is high above all the people.

Let them praise thy great and terrible name; for it is holy.

The king's strength also loveth judgment; thou dost establish equity, thou executest judgment and righteousness in Jacob.

Exalt ye the Lord our God, and worship at his footstool; for he is holy.

Moses and Aaron among his priests, and Samuel among them that call upon his name; they called upon the Lord, and he answered them.

He spake unto them in the cloudy pillar: they kept his testimonies, and the ordinance that he gave them.

Thou answeredst them, O Lord our God: thou wast a God that forgavest them, though thou tookest vengeance of their inventions.

Exalt the Lord our God, and worship at his holy hill; for the Lord our God is holy.

Like Moses, Aaron, and Samuel, call upon God
and let God answer you.

Psalm 100

Make a joyful noise unto the Lord, all ye lands.

Serve the Lord with gladness: come before his presence with
    singing.

Know ye that the Lord he is God: it is he that hath made us,
    and not we ourselves; we are his people, and the sheep of
    his pasture.

Enter into his gates with thanksgiving, and into his courts with
    praise: be thankful unto him, and bless his name.

For the Lord is good; his mercy is everlasting; and his truth
    endureth to all generations.

What holiday would this psalm be appropriate for?

'Psalm 101

I will sing of mercy and judgment: unto thee, O Lord, will I sing.

I will behave myself wisely in a perfect way. O when wilt thou come unto me? I will walk within my house with a perfect heart.

I will set no wicked thing before mine eyes: I hate the work of them that turn aside; it shall not cleave to me.

A froward heart shall depart from me: I will not know a wicked person.

Whoso privily slandereth his neighbor, him will I cut off: him that hath a high look and a proud heart will not I suffer.

Mine eyes shall be upon the faithful of the land, that they may dwell with me: he that walketh in a perfect way, he shall serve me.

He that worketh deceit shall not dwell within my house: he that telleth lies shall not tarry in my sight.

I will early destroy all the wicked of the land; that I may cut off all wicked doers from the city of the Lord.

"You are the company you keep." Stay with this idea throughout your day and see what it manifests.

Psalm 102

Hear my prayer, O Lord, and let my cry come unto thee.

Hide not thy face from me in the day when I am in trouble; incline thine ear unto me: in the day when I call answer me speedily.

For my days are consumed like smoke, and my bones are burned as a hearth.

My heart is smitten, and withered like grass; so that I forget to eat my bread.

By reason of the voice of my groaning my bones cleave to my skin.

I am like a pelican of the wilderness: I am like an owl of the desert.

I watch, and am as a sparrow alone upon the housetop.

Mine enemies reproach me all the day; and they that are mad against me are sworn against me.

For I have eaten ashes like bread, and mingled my drink with weeping,

Because of thine indignation and thy wrath: for thou hast lifted me up, and cast me down.

My days are like a shadow that declineth; and I am withered like grass.

But thou, O Lord, shalt endure forever; and thy remembrance unto all generations.

Thou shalt arise, and have mercy upon Zion: for the time to favor her, yea, the set time, is come.

For thy servants take pleasure in her stones, and favor the dust thereof.

So the heathen shall fear the name of the Lord, and all the kings of the earth thy glory.

When the Lord shall build up Zion, he shall appear in his glory.

He will regard the prayer of the destitute, and not despise their prayer,

This shall be written for the generation to come: and the people which shall be created shall praise the Lord.

For he hath looked down from the height of his sanctuary; from heaven did the Lord behold the earth;

To hear the groaning of the prisoner; to loose those that are appointed to death;

To declare the name of the Lord in Zion, and his praise in Jerusalem;

When the people are gathered together, and the kingdoms, to serve the Lord.

He weakened my strength in the way; he shortened my days.

I said, O my God, take me not away in the midst of my days: thy years are throughout all generations.

Of old hast thou laid the foundation of the earth: and the heavens are the work of thy hands.

They shall perish, but thou shalt endure: yea, all of them shall wax old like a garment; as a vesture shalt thou change them, and they shall be changed:

But thou art the same, and thy years shall have no end.

The children of thy servants shall continue, and their seed shall be established before thee.

———————

Do you feel this psalmist's lament? "I am like a pelican of the wilderness: I am like an owl of the desert. I . . . am as a sparrow alone upon the housetop. . . . I am withered like grass."

Psalm 103

Bless the Lord, O my soul: and all that is within me, bless his
holy name.

Bless the Lord, O my soul, and forget not all his benefits:

Who forgiveth all thine iniquities; who healeth all thy diseases;

Who redeemeth thy life from destruction; who crowneth thee
with loving-kindness and tender mercies;

Who satisfieth thy mouth with good things; so that thy youth is
renewed like the eagle's.

The Lord executeth righteousness and judgment for all that are
oppressed.

He made known his ways unto Moses, his acts unto the
children of Israel.

The Lord is merciful and gracious, slow to anger, and plenteous
in mercy.

He will not always chide: neither will he keep his anger forever.

He hath not dealt with us after our sins; nor rewarded us
according to our iniquities.

For as the heaven is high above the earth, so great is his mercy
toward them that fear him.

As far as the east is from the west, so far hath he removed our
transgressions from us.

Like as a father pitieth his children, so the Lord pitieth them
that fear him.

For he knoweth our frame; he remembereth that we are dust.

As for man, his days are as grass: as a flower of the field, so he
flourisheth.

For the wind passeth over it, and it is gone; and the place
thereof shall know it no more.

But the mercy of the Lord is from everlasting to everlasting
upon them that fear him, and his righteousness unto
children's children;

To such as keep his covenant, and to those that remember his
   commandments to do them.
The Lord hath prepared his throne in the heavens; and his
   kingdom ruleth over all.
Bless the Lord, ye his angels, that excel in strength, that do his
   commandments, hearkening unto the voice of his word.
Bless ye the Lord, all ye his hosts; ye ministers of his, that do his
   pleasure.
Bless the Lord, all his works in all places of his dominion: bless
   the Lord, O my soul.

*Watch and listen to the performance of "Bless the Lord" from
the musical Godspell. What feelings does it evoke?*

Psalm 104

Bless the Lord, O my soul. O Lord my God, thou art very great;
thou art clothed with honor and majesty:

Who coverest thyself with light as with a garment: who
stretchest out the heavens like a curtain:

Who layeth the beams of his chambers in the waters: who
maketh the clouds his chariot: who walketh upon the wings
of the wind:

Who maketh his angels spirits; his ministers a flaming fire:

Who laid the foundations of the earth, that it should not be
removed forever.

Thou coveredst it with the deep as with a garment: the waters
stood above the mountains.

At thy rebuke they fled; at the voice of thy thunder they hasted
away.

They go up by the mountains; they go down by the valleys
unto the place which thou hast founded for them.

Thou hast set a bound that they may not pass over; that they
turn not again to cover the earth.

He sendeth the springs into the valleys, which run among the
hills.

They give drink to every beast of the field: the wild asses
quench their thirst.

By them shall the fowls of the heaven have their habitation,
which sing among the branches.

He watereth the hills from his chambers: the earth is satisfied
with the fruit of thy works.

He causeth the grass to grow for the cattle, and herb for the
service of man: that he may bring forth food out of the
earth;

And wine that maketh glad the heart of man, and oil to make
his face to shine, and bread which strengtheneth man's
heart.

The trees of the Lord are full of sap; the cedars of Lebanon,
which he hath planted;

Where the birds make their nests: as for the stork, the fir trees
are her house.

The high hills are a refuge for the wild goats; and the rocks for
the conies.

He appointed the moon for seasons: the sun knoweth his going
down.

Thou makest darkness, and it is night: wherein all the beasts of
the forest do creep forth.

The young lions roar after their prey, and seek their meat from
God.

The sun ariseth, they gather themselves together, and lay them
down in their dens.

Man goeth forth unto his work and to his labor until the
evening.

O Lord, how manifold are thy works! in wisdom hast thou made
them all: the earth is full of thy riches.

So is this great and wide sea, wherein are things creeping
innumerable, both small and great beasts.

There go the ships: there is that leviathan, whom thou hast
made to play therein.

These wait all upon thee; that thou mayest give them their meat
in due season.

That thou givest them they gather: thou openest thine hand,
they are filled with good.

Thou hidest thy face, they are troubled: thou takest away their
breath, they die, and return to their dust.

Thou sendest forth thy spirit, they are created: and thou
renewest the face of the earth.

The glory of the Lord shall endure forever: the Lord shall
rejoice in his works.

He looketh on the earth, and it trembleth: he toucheth the hills,
and they smoke.

I will sing unto the Lord as long as I live: I will sing praise to my
   God while I have my being.
My meditation of him shall be sweet: I will be glad in the Lord.
Let the sinners be consumed out of the earth, and let the wicked
   be no more. Bless thou the Lord, O my soul. Praise ye the
   Lord.

What a celebration of creation and nature!
Recite this psalm for Earth Day, April 22.

‘Psalm 105

O give thanks unto the Lord; call upon his name: make known
his deeds among the people.

Sing unto him, sing psalms unto him: talk ye of all his wondrous
works.

Glory ye in his holy name: let the heart of them rejoice that
seek the Lord.

Seek the Lord, and his strength: seek his face evermore.

Remember his marvelous works that he hath done; his wonders,
and the judgments of his mouth;

O ye seed of Abraham his servant, ye children of Jacob his
chosen.

He is the Lord our God: his judgments are in all the earth.

He hath remembered his covenant forever, the word which he
commanded to a thousand generations.

Which covenant he made with Abraham, and his oath unto
Isaac;

And confirmed the same unto Jacob for a law, and to Israel for
an everlasting covenant:

Saying, Unto thee will I give the land of Canaan, the lot of your
inheritance:

When they were but a few men in number; yea, very few, and
strangers in it.

When they went from one nation to another, from one
kingdom to another people;

He suffered no man to do them wrong: yea, he reproved kings
for their sakes;

Saying, Touch not mine anointed, and do my prophets no harm.

Moreover he called for a famine upon the land: he brake the
whole staff of bread.

He sent a man before them, even Joseph, who was sold for a
servant:

Whose feet they hurt with fetters: he was laid in iron:

Until the time that his word came: the word of the Lord tried him.

The king sent and loosed him; even the ruler of the people, and let him go free.

He made him lord of his house, and ruler of all his substance:

To bind his princes at his pleasure; and teach his senators wisdom.

Israel also came into Egypt; and Jacob sojourned in the land of Ham.

And he increased his people greatly; and made them stronger than their enemies.

He turned their heart to hate his people, to deal subtilely with his servants.

He sent Moses his servant; and Aaron whom he had chosen.

They showed his signs among them, and wonders in the land of Ham.

He sent darkness, and made it dark; and they rebelled not against his word.

He turned their waters into blood, and slew their fish.

Their land brought forth frogs in abundance, in the chambers of their kings.

He spake, and there came divers sorts of flies, and lice in all their coasts.

He gave them hail for rain, and flaming fire in their land.

He smote their vines also and their fig trees; and brake the trees of their coasts.

He spake, and the locusts came, and caterpillars, and that without number,

And did eat up all the herbs in their land, and devoured the fruit of their ground.

He smote also all the firstborn in their land, the chief of all their strength.

He brought them forth also with silver and gold: and there was not one feeble person among their tribes.

Egypt was glad when they departed: for the fear of them fell upon them.

He spread a cloud for a covering; and fire to give light in the night.

The people asked, and he brought quails, and satisfied them with the bread of heaven.

He opened the rock, and the waters gushed out; they ran in the dry places like a river.

For he remembered his holy promise, and Abraham his servant.

And he brought forth his people with joy, and his chosen with gladness:

And gave them the lands of the heathen: and they inherited the labor of the people;

That they might observe his statutes, and keep his laws. Praise ye the Lord.

Imagine the female counterparts of all the male characters named in this psalm and how that would change the complexion of the story (Sarah/Abraham, Leah/Rachel/Jacob, Rebekah/Isaac, Asenath/Joseph, Na'eltama'uk/Ham).

Psalm 106

Praise ye the Lord. O give thanks unto the Lord; for he is good:
  for his mercy endureth forever.

Who can utter the mighty acts of the Lord? who can show forth
  all his praise?

Blessed are they that keep judgment, and he that doeth
  righteousness at all times.

Remember me, O Lord, with the favor that thou bearest unto
  thy people: O visit me with thy salvation;

That I may see the good of thy chosen, that I may rejoice in
  the gladness of thy nation, that I may glory with thine
  inheritance.

We have sinned with our fathers, we have committed iniquity,
  we have done wickedly.

Our fathers understood not thy wonders in Egypt; they
  remembered not the multitude of thy mercies; but
  provoked him at the sea, even at the Red sea.

Nevertheless he saved them for his name's sake, that he might
  make his mighty power to be known.

He rebuked the Red sea also, and it was dried up: so he led
  them through the depths, as through the wilderness.

And he saved them from the hand of him that hated them, and
  redeemed them from the hand of the enemy.

And the waters covered their enemies: there was not one of
  them left.

Then believed they his words; they sang his praise.

They soon forgat his works; they waited not for his counsel:

But lusted exceedingly in the wilderness, and tempted God in
  the desert.

And he gave them their request; but sent leanness into their
  soul.

They envied Moses also in the camp, and Aaron the saint of the
  Lord.

The earth opened and swallowed up Dathan, and covered the company of Abiram.

And a fire was kindled in their company; the flame burned up the wicked.

They made a calf in Horeb, and worshipped the molten image.

Thus they changed their glory into the similitude of an ox that eateth grass.

They forgat God their saviour, which had done great things in Egypt;

Wondrous works in the land of Ham, and terrible things by the Red sea.

Therefore he said that he would destroy them, had not Moses his chosen stood before him in the breach, to turn away his wrath, lest he should destroy them.

Yea, they despised the pleasant land, they believed not his word:

But murmured in their tents, and hearkened not unto the voice of the Lord.

Therefore he lifted up his hand against them, to overthrow them in the wilderness:

To overthrow their seed also among the nations, and to scatter them in the lands.

They joined themselves also unto Baalpeor, and ate the sacrifices of the dead.

Thus they provoked him to anger with their inventions: and the plague brake in upon them.

Then stood up Phinehas, and executed judgment: and so the plague was stayed.

And that was counted unto him for righteousness unto all generations forevermore.

They angered him also at the waters of strife, so that it went ill with Moses for their sakes:

Because they provoked his spirit, so that he spake unadvisedly with his lips.

They did not destroy the nations, concerning whom the Lord
    commanded them:
But were mingled among the heathen, and learned their works.
And they served their idols: which were a snare unto them.
Yea, they sacrificed their sons and their daughters unto devils,
And shed innocent blood, even the blood of their sons and of
    their daughters, whom they sacrificed unto the idols of
    Canaan: and the land was polluted with blood.
Thus were they defiled with their own works, and went a
    whoring with their own inventions.
Therefore was the wrath of the Lord kindled against his people,
    insomuch that he abhorred his own inheritance.
And he gave them into the hand of the heathen; and they that
    hated them ruled over them.
Their enemies also oppressed them, and they were brought into
    subjection under their hand.
Many times did he deliver them; but they provoked him with
    their counsel, and were brought low for their iniquity.
Nevertheless he regarded their affliction, when he heard their
    cry:
And he remembered for them his covenant, and repented
    according to the multitude of his mercies.
He made them also to be pitied of all those that carried them
    captives.
Save us, O Lord our God, and gather us from among the
    heathen, to give thanks unto thy holy name, and to triumph
    in thy praise.
Blessed be the Lord God of Israel from everlasting to
    everlasting: and let all the people say, Amen. Praise ye the
    Lord.

*The last psalm of Book 4 recounts the story of Moses
and his people. What parallels of this ancient tale with that of
current-day humanity do you recognize?*

_____

_____

_____

_____

_____

_____

_____

Psalm 107

O give thanks unto the Lord, for he is good: for his mercy
endureth forever.

Let the redeemed of the Lord say so, whom he hath redeemed
from the hand of the enemy;

And gathered them out of the lands, from the east, and from the
west, from the north, and from the south.

They wandered in the wilderness in a solitary way; they found
no city to dwell in.

Hungry and thirsty, their soul fainted in them.

Then they cried unto the Lord in their trouble, and he delivered
them out of their distresses.

And he led them forth by the right way, that they might go to a
city of habitation.

Oh that men would praise the Lord for his goodness, and for his
wonderful works to the children of men!

For he satisfieth the longing soul, and filleth the hungry soul
with goodness.

Such as sit in darkness and in the shadow of death, being bound
in affliction and iron;

Because they rebelled against the words of God, and contemned
the counsel of the Most High:

Therefore he brought down their heart with labor; they fell
down, and there was none to help.

Then they cried unto the Lord in their trouble, and he saved
them out of their distresses.

He brought them out of darkness and the shadow of death, and
brake their bands in sunder.

Oh that men would praise the Lord for his goodness, and for his
wonderful works to the children of men!

For he hath broken the gates of brass, and cut the bars of iron in
sunder.

Fools, because of their transgression, and because of their
iniquities, are afflicted.

Their soul abhorreth all manner of meat; and they draw near
unto the gates of death.

Then they cry unto the Lord in their trouble, and he saveth
them out of their distresses.

He sent his word, and healed them, and delivered them from
their destructions.

Oh that men would praise the Lord for his goodness, and for his
wonderful works to the children of men!

And let them sacrifice the sacrifices of thanksgiving, and declare
his works with rejoicing.

They that go down to the sea in ships, that do business in great waters;

These see the works of the Lord, and his wonders in the deep.

For he commandeth, and raiseth the stormy wind, which lifteth
up the waves thereof.

They mount up to the heaven, they go down again to the
depths: their soul is melted because of trouble.

They reel to and fro, and stagger like a drunken man, and are at
their wit's end.

Then they cry unto the Lord in their trouble, and he bringeth
them out of their distresses.

He maketh the storm a calm, so that the waves thereof are still.

Then are they glad because they be quiet; so he bringeth them
unto their desired haven.

Oh that men would praise the Lord for his goodness, and for his
wonderful works to the children of men!

Let them exalt him also in the congregation of the people, and
praise him in the assembly of the elders.

He turneth rivers into a wilderness, and the watersprings into
dry ground;

A fruitful land into barrenness, for the wickedness of them that
dwell therein.

He turneth the wilderness into a standing water, and dry ground
 into watersprings.
And there he maketh the hungry to dwell, that they may
 prepare a city for habitation;
And sow the fields, and plant vineyards, which may yield fruits
 of increase.
He blesseth them also, so that they are multiplied greatly; and
 suffereth not their cattle to decrease.
Again, they are minished and brought low through oppression,
 affliction, and sorrow.
He poureth contempt upon princes, and causeth them to
 wander in the wilderness, where there is no way.
Yet setteth he the poor on high from affliction, and maketh him
 families like a flock.
The righteous shall see it, and rejoice: and all iniquity shall stop
 her mouth.
Whoso is wise, and will observe these things, even they shall
 understand the loving-kindness of the Lord.

How does the refrain of the first psalm of Book 5 make you feel?
"Oh that men would praise the Lord for his goodness, and for his
wonderful works to the children of men!"

Psalm 108

O God, my heart is fixed; I will sing and give praise, even with my glory.

Awake, psaltery and harp: I myself will awake early.

I will praise thee, O Lord, among the people: and I will sing praises unto thee among the nations.

For thy mercy is great above the heavens: and thy truth reacheth unto the clouds.

Be thou exalted, O God, above the heavens: and thy glory above all the earth;

That thy beloved may be delivered: save with thy right hand, and answer me.

God hath spoken in his holiness; I will rejoice, I will divide Shechem, and mete out the valley of Succoth.

Gilead is mine; Manasseh is mine; Ephraim also is the strength of mine head; Judah is my lawgiver;

Moab is my washpot; over Edom will I cast out my shoe; over Philistia will I triumph.

Who will bring me into the strong city? who will lead me into Edom?

Wilt not thou, O God, who hast cast us off? and wilt not thou, O God, go forth with our hosts?

Give us help from trouble: for vain is the help of man.

Through God we shall do valiantly: for he it is that shall tread down our enemies.

The "Prince of Preachers," Charles Spurgeon, referred to this psalm as "The Warrior's Morning Song." Imagine how this would prepare you for the day's conflict.

Psalm 109

Hold not thy peace, O God of my praise;

For the mouth of the wicked and the mouth of the deceitful are
opened against me: they have spoken against me with a
lying tongue.

They compassed me about also with words of hatred; and
fought against me without a cause.

For my love they are my adversaries: but I give myself unto prayer.

And they have rewarded me evil for good, and hatred for my love.

Set thou a wicked man over him: and let Satan stand at his right
hand.

When he shall be judged, let him be condemned: and let his
prayer become sin.

Let his days be few; and let another take his office.

Let his children be fatherless, and his wife a widow.

Let his children be continually vagabonds, and beg: let them
seek their bread also out of their desolate places.

Let the extortioner catch all that he hath; and let the strangers
spoil his labor.

Let there be none to extend mercy unto him: neither let there
be any to favor his fatherless children.

Let his posterity be cut off; and in the generation following let
their name be blotted out.

Let the iniquity of his fathers be remembered with the Lord;
and let not the sin of his mother be blotted out.

Let them be before the Lord continually, that he may cut off the
memory of them from the earth.

Because that he remembered not to show mercy, but persecuted
the poor and needy man, that he might even slay the
broken in heart.

As he loved cursing, so let it come unto him: as he delighted
not in blessing, so let it be far from him.

As he clothed himself with cursing like as with his garment, so let
it come into his bowels like water, and like oil into his bones.

Let it be unto him as the garment which covereth him, and for a
girdle wherewith he is girded continually.

Let this be the reward of mine adversaries from the Lord, and of
them that speak evil against my soul.

But do thou for me, O God the Lord, for thy name's sake:
because thy mercy is good, deliver thou me.

For I am poor and needy, and my heart is wounded within me.

I am gone like the shadow when it declineth: I am tossed up and
down as the locust.

My knees are weak through fasting; and my flesh faileth of fatness.

I became also a reproach unto them: when they looked upon me
they shook their heads.

Help me, O Lord my God: O save me according to thy mercy:

That they may know that this is thy hand; that thou, Lord, hast
done it.

Let them curse, but bless thou: when they arise, let them be
ashamed; but let thy servant rejoice.

Let mine adversaries be clothed with shame; and let them cover
themselves with their own confusion, as with a mantle.

I will greatly praise the Lord with my mouth; yea, I will praise
him among the multitude.

For he shall stand at the right hand of the poor, to save him
from those that condemn his soul.

---

*What do you think about all these graphic curses that this psalm
wishes upon one's enemies? Is this a constructive way of thinking?*

_____

_____

_____

_____

Psalm 110

The Lord said unto my Lord, Sit thou at my right hand, until I
    make thine enemies thy footstool.

The Lord shall send the rod of thy strength out of Zion: rule
    thou in the midst of thine enemies.

Thy people shall be willing in the day of thy power, in the
    beauties of holiness from the womb of the morning: thou
    hast the dew of thy youth.

The Lord hath sworn, and will not repent, Thou art a priest
    forever after the order of Melchizedek.

The Lord at thy right hand shall strike through kings in the day
    of his wrath.

He shall judge among the heathen, he shall fill the places with
    the dead bodies; he shall wound the heads over many
    countries.

He shall drink of the brook in the way: therefore shall he lift up
    the head.

Find a phrase of beauty in this psalm.

Psalm 111

Praise ye the Lord. I will praise the Lord with my whole heart,
    in the assembly of the upright, and in the congregation.
The works of the Lord are great, sought out of all them that
    have pleasure therein.
His work is honorable and glorious: and his righteousness
    endureth forever.
He hath made his wonderful works to be remembered: the Lord
    is gracious and full of compassion.
He hath given meat unto them that fear him: he will ever be
    mindful of his covenant.
He hath showed his people the power of his works, that he may
    give them the heritage of the heathen.
The works of his hands are verity and judgment; all his
    commandments are sure.
They stand fast forever and ever, and are done in truth and
    uprightness.
He sent redemption unto his people: he hath commanded his
    covenant forever: holy and reverend is his name.
The fear of the Lord is the beginning of wisdom: a good
    understanding have all they that do his commandments: his
    praise endureth forever.

---

*This psalm is an acrostic poem, the lines of which begin with the
successive letters of the Hebrew alphabet. Create your
own ten-verse acrostic poem, using the English alphabet.*

Psalm 112

Praise ye the Lord. Blessed is the man that feareth the Lord, that
delighteth greatly in his commandments.

His seed shall be mighty upon earth: the generation of the
upright shall be blessed.

Wealth and riches shall be in his house: and his righteousness
endureth forever.

Unto the upright there ariseth light in the darkness: he is
gracious, and full of compassion, and righteous.

A good man showeth favor, and lendeth: he will guide his affairs
with discretion.

Surely he shall not be moved forever: the righteous shall be in
everlasting remembrance.

He shall not be afraid of evil tidings: his heart is fixed, trusting
in the Lord.

His heart is established, he shall not be afraid, until he see his
desire upon his enemies.

He hath dispersed, he hath given to the poor; his righteousness
endureth forever; his horn shall be exalted with honor.

The wicked shall see it, and be grieved; he shall gnash with his
teeth, and melt away: the desire of the wicked shall perish.

This psalm mentions righteousness several times.
What does righteousness mean to you?

Psalm 113

Praise ye the Lord. Praise, O ye servants of the Lord, praise the name of the Lord.

Blessed be the name of the Lord from this time forth and forevermore.

From the rising of the sun unto the going down of the same the Lord's name is to be praised.

The Lord is high above all nations, and his glory above the heavens.

Who is like unto the Lord our God, who dwelleth on high,

Who humbleth himself to behold the things that are in heaven, and in the earth!

He raiseth up the poor out of the dust, and lifteth the needy out of the dunghill;

That he may set him with princes, even with the princes of his people.

He maketh the barren woman to keep house, and to be a joyful mother of children. Praise ye the Lord.

Psalm 113 and the following five psalms are referred to in the Talmud as "the Hallel" or "praises," and they are considered to be a single composition. Read Psalms 113, 114, 115, 116, 117, and 118 straight through and consider why they may have been separated in the way they were.

Psalm 114

When Israel went out of Egypt, the house of Jacob from a
    people of strange language;
Judah was his sanctuary, and Israel his dominion.
The sea saw it, and fled: Jordan was driven back.
The mountains skipped like rams, and the little hills like lambs.
What ailed thee, O thou sea, that thou fleddest? thou Jordan,
    that thou wast driven back?
Ye mountains, that ye skipped like rams; and ye little hills, like
    lambs?
Tremble, thou earth, at the presence of the Lord, at the
    presence of the God of Jacob;
Which turned the rock into a standing water, the flint into a
    fountain of waters.

Psalm 115

Not unto us, O Lord, not unto us, but unto thy name give glory,
    for thy mercy, and for thy truth's sake.
Wherefore should the heathen say, Where is now their God?
But our God is in the heavens: he hath done whatsoever he hath
    pleased.
Their idols are silver and gold, the work of men's hands.
They have mouths, but they speak not: eyes have they, but they
    see not:
They have ears, but they hear not: noses have they, but they
    smell not:
They have hands, but they handle not: feet have they, but they
    walk not: neither speak they through their throat.
They that make them are like unto them; so is every one that
    trusteth in them.

O Israel, trust thou in the Lord: he is their help and their shield.

O house of Aaron, trust in the Lord: he is their help and their
shield.

Ye that fear the Lord, trust in the Lord: he is their help and their
shield.

The Lord hath been mindful of us: he will bless us; he will bless
the house of Israel; he will bless the house of Aaron.

He will bless them that fear the Lord, both small and great.

The Lord shall increase you more and more, you and your
children.

Ye are blessed of the Lord which made heaven and earth.

The heaven, even the heavens, are the Lord's: but the earth hath
he given to the children of men.

The dead praise not the Lord, neither any that go down into
silence.

But we will bless the Lord from this time forth and forevermore.
Praise the Lord.

Psalm 116

I love the Lord, because he hath heard my voice and my
supplications.

Because he hath inclined his ear unto me, therefore will I call
upon him as long as I live.

The sorrows of death compassed me, and the pains of hell gat
hold upon me: I found trouble and sorrow.

Then called I upon the name of the Lord; O Lord, I beseech
thee, deliver my soul.

Gracious is the Lord, and righteous; yea, our God is merciful.

The Lord preserveth the simple: I was brought low, and he
helped me.

Return unto thy rest, O my soul; for the Lord hath dealt
    bountifully with thee.
For thou hast delivered my soul from death, mine eyes from
    tears, and my feet from falling.
I will walk before the Lord in the land of the living.
I believed, therefore have I spoken: I was greatly afflicted:
I said in my haste, All men are liars.
What shall I render unto the Lord for all his benefits toward me?
I will take the cup of salvation, and call upon the name of the
    Lord.
I will pay my vows unto the Lord now in the presence of all his
    people.
Precious in the sight of the Lord is the death of his saints.
O Lord, truly I am thy servant; I am thy servant, and the son of
    thine handmaid: thou hast loosed my bonds.
I will offer to thee the sacrifice of thanksgiving, and will call
    upon the name of the Lord.
I will pay my vows unto the Lord now in the presence of all his
    people,
In the courts of the Lord's house, in the midst of thee,
    O Jerusalem. Praise ye the Lord.

Psalm 117

O praise the Lord, all ye nations: praise him, all ye people.
For his merciful kindness is great toward us: and the truth of the
    Lord endureth forever. Praise ye the Lord.

Psalm 118

O give thanks unto the Lord; for he is good: because his mercy
    endureth forever.

Let Israel now say, that his mercy endureth forever.

Let the house of Aaron now say, that his mercy endureth
    forever.

Let them now that fear the Lord say, that his mercy endureth
    forever.

I called upon the Lord in distress: the Lord answered me, and
    set me in a large place.

The Lord is on my side; I will not fear: what can man do unto
    me?

The Lord taketh my part with them that help me: therefore
    shall I see my desire upon them that hate me.

It is better to trust in the Lord than to put confidence in man.

It is better to trust in the Lord than to put confidence in princes.

All nations compassed me about: but in the name of the Lord
    will I destroy them.

They compassed me about; yea, they compassed me about: but
    in the name of the Lord I will destroy them.

They compassed me about like bees; they are quenched as the
    fire of thorns: for in the name of the Lord I will destroy
    them.

Thou hast thrust sore at me that I might fall: but the Lord
    helped me.

The Lord is my strength and song, and is become my salvation.

The voice of rejoicing and salvation is in the tabernacles of the
    righteous: the right hand of the Lord doeth valiantly.

The right hand of the Lord is exalted: the right hand of the
    Lord doeth valiantly.

I shall not die, but live, and declare the works of the Lord.

The Lord hath chastened me sore: but he hath not given me
    over unto death.

Open to me the gates of righteousness: I will go into them, and
I will praise the Lord:
This gate of the Lord, into which the righteous shall enter.
I will praise thee: for thou hast heard me, and art become my
salvation.
The stone which the builders refused is become the head stone
of the corner.
This is the Lord's doing; it is marvelous in our eyes.
This is the day which the Lord hath made; we will rejoice and
be glad in it.
Save now, I beseech thee, O Lord: O Lord, I beseech thee, send
now prosperity.
Blessed be he that cometh in the name of the Lord: we have
blessed you out of the house of the Lord.
God is the Lord, which hath showed us light: bind the sacrifice
with cords, even unto the horns of the altar.
Thou art my God, and I will praise thee: thou art my God, I will
exalt thee.
O give thanks unto the Lord; for he is good: for his mercy
endureth forever.

'Psalm 119

ALEPH

Blessed are the undefiled in the way, who walk in the law of the
Lord.
Blessed are they that keep his testimonies, and that seek him
with the whole heart.
They also do no iniquity: they walk in his ways.
Thou hast commanded us to keep thy precepts diligently.
O that my ways were directed to keep thy statutes!
Then shall I not be ashamed, when I have respect unto all thy
commandments.
I will praise thee with uprightness of heart, when I shall have
learned thy righteous judgments.
I will keep thy statutes: O forsake me not utterly.

BETH

Wherewithal shall a young man cleanse his way? by taking heed
thereto according to thy word.
With my whole heart have I sought thee: O let me not wander
from thy commandments.
Thy word have I hid in mine heart, that I might not sin against thee.
Blessed art thou, O Lord: teach me thy statutes.
With my lips have I declared all the judgments of thy mouth.
I have rejoiced in the way of thy testimonies, as much as in all riches.
I will meditate in thy precepts, and have respect unto thy ways.
I will delight myself in thy statutes: I will not forget thy word.

GIMEL

Deal bountifully with thy servant, that I may live, and keep thy word.
Open thou mine eyes, that I may behold wondrous things out
of thy law.

I am a stranger in the earth: hide not thy commandments from me.

My soul breaketh for the longing that it hath unto thy
    judgments at all times.

Thou hast rebuked the proud that are cursed, which do err from
    thy commandments.

Remove from me reproach and contempt; for I have kept thy
    testimonies.

Princes also did sit and speak against me: but thy servant did
    meditate in thy statutes.

Thy testimonies also are my delight, and my counselors.

DALETH

My soul cleaveth unto the dust: quicken thou me according to
    thy word.

I have declared my ways, and thou heardest me: teach me thy
    statutes.

Make me to understand the way of thy precepts: so shall I talk
    of thy wondrous works.

My soul melteth for heaviness: strengthen thou me according
    unto thy word.

Remove from me the way of lying: and grant me thy law graciously.

I have chosen the way of truth: thy judgments have I laid before me.

I have stuck unto thy testimonies: O Lord, put me not to shame.

I will run the way of thy commandments, when thou shalt
    enlarge my heart.

HE

Teach me, O Lord, the way of thy statutes; and I shall keep it
    unto the end.

Give me understanding, and I shall keep thy law; yea, I shall
    observe it with my whole heart.

Make me to go in the path of thy commandments; for therein
    do I delight.

Incline my heart unto thy testimonies, and not to covetousness.

Turn away mine eyes from beholding vanity; and quicken thou me in thy way.

Stablish thy word unto thy servant, who is devoted to thy fear.

Turn away my reproach which I fear: for thy judgments are good.

Behold, I have longed after thy precepts: quicken me in thy righteousness.

VAU

Let thy mercies come also unto me, O Lord, even thy salvation, according to thy word.

So shall I have wherewith to answer him that reproacheth me: for I trust in thy word.

And take not the word of truth utterly out of my mouth; for I have hoped in thy judgments.

So shall I keep thy law continually forever and ever.

And I will walk at liberty: for I seek thy precepts.

I will speak of thy testimonies also before kings, and will not be ashamed.

And I will delight myself in thy commandments, which I have loved.

My hands also will I lift up unto thy commandments, which I have loved; and I will meditate in thy statutes.

ZAIN

Remember the word unto thy servant, upon which thou hast caused me to hope.

This is my comfort in my affliction: for thy word hath quickened me.

The proud have had me greatly in derision: yet have I not declined from thy law.

I remembered thy judgments of old, O Lord; and have comforted myself.

Horror hath taken hold upon me because of the wicked that
    forsake thy law.
Thy statutes have been my songs in the house of my pilgrimage.
I have remembered thy name, O Lord, in the night, and have
    kept thy law.
This I had, because I kept thy precepts.

CHETH

Thou art my portion, O Lord: I have said that I would keep thy
    words.
I entreated thy favor with my whole heart: be merciful unto me
    according to thy word.
I thought on my ways, and turned my feet unto thy testimonies.
I made haste, and delayed not to keep thy commandments.
The bands of the wicked have robbed me: but I have not
    forgotten thy law.
At midnight I will rise to give thanks unto thee because of thy
    righteous judgments.
I am a companion of all them that fear thee, and of them that
    keep thy precepts.
The earth, O Lord, is full of thy mercy: teach me thy statutes.

TETH

Thou hast dealt well with thy servant, O Lord, according unto
    thy word.
Teach me good judgment and knowledge: for I have believed
    thy commandments.
Before I was afflicted I went astray: but now have I kept thy word.
Thou art good, and doest good: teach me thy statutes.
The proud have forged a lie against me: but I will keep thy
    precepts with my whole heart.
Their heart is as fat as grease: but I delight in thy law.

It is good for me that I have been afflicted; that I might learn
thy statutes.
The law of thy mouth is better unto me than thousands of gold
and silver.

JOD

Thy hands have made me and fashioned me: give me
understanding, that I may learn thy commandments.
They that fear thee will be glad when they see me; because I
have hoped in thy word.
I know, O Lord, that thy judgments are right, and that thou in
faithfulness hast afflicted me.
Let, I pray thee, thy merciful kindness be for my comfort,
according to thy word unto thy servant.
Let thy tender mercies come unto me, that I may live: for thy
law is my delight.
Let the proud be ashamed; for they dealt perversely with me
without a cause: but I will meditate in thy precepts.
Let those that fear thee turn unto me, and those that have
known thy testimonies.
Let my heart be sound in thy statutes; that I be not ashamed.

CAPH

My soul fainteth for thy salvation: but I hope in thy word.
Mine eyes fail for thy word, saying, When wilt thou comfort
me?
For I am become like a bottle in the smoke; yet do I not forget
thy statutes.
How many are the days of thy servant? when wilt thou execute
judgment on them that persecute me?
The proud have digged pits for me, which are not after thy law.
All thy commandments are faithful: they persecute me
wrongfully; help thou me.

They had almost consumed me upon earth; but I forsook not
    thy precepts.

Quicken me after thy loving-kindness; so shall I keep the
    testimony of thy mouth.

LAMED

Forever, O Lord, thy word is settled in heaven.

Thy faithfulness is unto all generations: thou hast established
    the earth, and it abideth.

They continue this day according to thine ordinances: for all
    are thy servants.

Unless thy law had been my delights, I should then have
    perished in mine affliction.

I will never forget thy precepts: for with them thou hast
    quickened me.

I am thine, save me; for I have sought thy precepts.

The wicked have waited for me to destroy me: but I will
    consider thy testimonies.

I have seen an end of all perfection: but thy commandment is
    exceeding broad.

MEM

O how love I thy law! it is my meditation all the day.

Thou through thy commandments hast made me wiser than
    mine enemies: for they are ever with me.

I have more understanding than all my teachers: for thy
    testimonies are my meditation.

I understand more than the ancients, because I keep thy
    precepts.

I have refrained my feet from every evil way, that I might keep
    thy word.

I have not departed from thy judgments: for thou hast taught me.

How sweet are thy words unto my taste! yea, sweeter than
honey to my mouth.

Through thy precepts I get understanding: therefore I hate
every false way.

NUN

Thy word is a lamp unto my feet, and a light unto my path.

I have sworn, and I will perform it, that I will keep thy righteous
judgments.

I am afflicted very much: quicken me, O Lord, according unto
thy word.

Accept, I beseech thee, the freewill offerings of my mouth,
O Lord, and teach me thy judgments.

My soul is continually in my hand: yet do I not forget thy law.

The wicked have laid a snare for me: yet I erred not from thy
precepts.

Thy testimonies have I taken as a heritage forever: for they are
the rejoicing of my heart.

I have inclined mine heart to perform thy statutes always, even
unto the end.

SAMECH

I hate vain thoughts: but thy law do I love.

Thou art my hiding place and my shield: I hope in thy word.

Depart from me, ye evildoers: for I will keep the
commandments of my God.

Uphold me according unto thy word, that I may live: and let me
not be ashamed of my hope.

Hold thou me up, and I shall be safe: and I will have respect
unto thy statutes continually.

Thou hast trodden down all them that err from thy statutes: for
their deceit is falsehood.

Thou puttest away all the wicked of the earth like dross:
  therefore I love thy testimonies.
My flesh trembleth for fear of thee; and I am afraid of thy
  judgments.

AIN

I have done judgment and justice: leave me not to mine
  oppressors.
Be surety for thy servant for good: let not the proud oppress me.
Mine eyes fail for thy salvation, and for the word of thy
  righteousness.
Deal with thy servant according unto thy mercy, and teach me
  thy statutes.
I am thy servant; give me understanding, that I may know thy
  testimonies.
It is time for thee, Lord, to work: for they have made void thy law.
Therefore I love thy commandments above gold; yea, above
  fine gold.
Therefore I esteem all thy precepts concerning all things to be
  right; and I hate every false way.

PE

Thy testimonies are wonderful: therefore doth my soul keep
  them.
The entrance of thy words giveth light; it giveth understanding
  unto the simple.
I opened my mouth, and panted: for I longed for thy
  commandments.
Look thou upon me, and be merciful unto me, as thou usest to
  do unto those that love thy name.
Order my steps in thy word: and let not any iniquity have
  dominion over me.

Deliver me from the oppression of man: so will I keep thy
   precepts.
Make thy face to shine upon thy servant; and teach me thy
   statutes.
Rivers of waters run down mine eyes, because they keep not thy
   law.

TZADDI

Righteous art thou, O Lord, and upright are thy judgments.
Thy testimonies that thou hast commanded are righteous and
   very faithful.
My zeal hath consumed me, because mine enemies have
   forgotten thy words.
Thy word is very pure: therefore thy servant loveth it.
I am small and despised: yet do not I forget thy precepts.
Thy righteousness is an everlasting righteousness, and thy law is
   the truth.
Trouble and anguish have taken hold on me: yet thy
   commandments are my delights.
The righteousness of thy testimonies is everlasting: give me
   understanding, and I shall live.

KOPH

I cried with my whole heart; hear me, O Lord: I will keep thy
   statutes.
I cried unto thee; save me, and I shall keep thy testimonies.
I prevented the dawning of the morning, and cried: I hoped in
   thy word.
Mine eyes prevent the night watches, that I might meditate in
   thy word.
Hear my voice according unto thy loving-kindness: O Lord,
   quicken me according to thy judgment.

They draw nigh that follow after mischief: they are far from thy
law.

Thou art near, O Lord; and all thy commandments are truth.

Concerning thy testimonies, I have known of old that thou hast
founded them forever.

RESH

Consider mine affliction, and deliver me: for I do not forget thy
law.

Plead my cause, and deliver me: quicken me according to thy
word.

Salvation is far from the wicked: for they seek not thy statutes.

Great are thy tender mercies, O Lord: quicken me according to
thy judgments.

Many are my persecutors and mine enemies; yet do I not
decline from thy testimonies.

I beheld the transgressors, and was grieved; because they kept
not thy word.

Consider how I love thy precepts: quicken me, O Lord,
according to thy loving-kindness.

Thy word is true from the beginning: and every one of thy
righteous judgments endureth forever.

SCHIN

Princes have persecuted me without a cause: but my heart
standeth in awe of thy word.

I rejoice at thy word, as one that findeth great spoil.

I hate and abhor lying: but thy law do I love.

Seven times a day do I praise thee, because of thy righteous
judgments.

Great peace have they which love thy law: and nothing shall
offend them.

Lord, I have hoped for thy salvation, and done thy
commandments.
My soul hath kept thy testimonies; and I love them exceedingly.
I have kept thy precepts and thy testimonies: for all my ways
are before thee.

TAU

Let my cry come near before thee, O Lord: give me
understanding according to thy word.
Let my supplication come before thee: deliver me according to
thy word.
My lips shall utter praise, when thou hast taught me thy
statutes.
My tongue shall speak of thy word: for all thy commandments
are righteousness.
Let thine hand help me; for I have chosen thy precepts.
I have longed for thy salvation, O Lord; and thy law is my
delight.
Let my soul live, and it shall praise thee; and let thy judgments
help me.
I have gone astray like a lost sheep: seek thy servant; for I do
not forget thy commandments.

———

*This is the longest psalm, the longest chapter in the Bible, and an
acrostic poem (each stanza begins with a subsequent letter of the
Hebrew alphabet). What stands out to you in this epic psalm?*

———

———

———

Psalm 120

In my distress I cried unto the Lord, and he heard me.

Deliver my soul, O Lord, from lying lips, and from a deceitful
tongue.

What shall be given unto thee? or what shall be done unto thee,
thou false tongue?

Sharp arrows of the mighty, with coals of juniper.

Woe is me, that I sojourn in Mesech, that I dwell in the tents of
Kedar!

My soul hath long dwelt with him that hateth peace.

I am for peace: but when I speak, they are for war.

---

*This and the following fourteen psalms are sometimes called
"the Pilgrim Songs," which were sung as people went to Jerusalem
to attend three annual pilgrim festivals. Familiarize yourself with
Passover, Shavuot, and Sukkot and their meanings.*

Psalm 121

I will lift up mine eyes unto the hills, from whence cometh my
   help.
My help cometh from the Lord, which made heaven and earth.
He will not suffer thy foot to be moved: he that keepeth thee
   will not slumber.
Behold, he that keepeth Israel shall neither slumber nor sleep.
The Lord is thy keeper: the Lord is thy shade upon thy right
   hand.
The sun shall not smite thee by day, nor the moon by night.
The Lord shall preserve thee from all evil: he shall preserve thy
   soul.
The Lord shall preserve thy going out and thy coming in from
   this time forth, and even forevermore.

*Listen to the second movement of "Mass" by Leonard Bernstein,
which he based on this psalm. Have you heard this piece before?
How does it make you feel?*

Psalm 122

I was glad when they said unto me, Let us go into the house of
the Lord.
Our feet shall stand within thy gates, O Jerusalem.
Jerusalem is builded as a city that is compact together:
Whither the tribes go up, the tribes of the Lord, unto the
testimony of Israel, to give thanks unto the name of the
Lord.
For there are set thrones of judgment, the thrones of the house
of David.
Pray for the peace of Jerusalem: they shall prosper that love
thee.
Peace be within thy walls, and prosperity within thy palaces.
For my brethren and companions' sakes, I will now say, Peace be
within thee.
Because of the house of the Lord our God I will seek thy good.

What comes to mind when you read "Peace be within thee"?

Psalm 123

Unto thee lift I up mine eyes, O thou that dwellest in the heavens.

Behold, as the eyes of servants look unto the hand of their masters, and as the eyes of a maiden unto the hand of her mistress; so our eyes wait upon the Lord our God, until that he have mercy upon us.

Have mercy upon us, O Lord, have mercy upon us: for we are exceedingly filled with contempt.

Our soul is exceedingly filled with the scorning of those that are at ease, and with the contempt of the proud.

There are a number of contemporary songs based on this psalm.
Search for them, pick one to listen to, and enjoy.

Psalm 124

If it had not been the Lord who was on our side, now may Israel say;

If it had not been the Lord who was on our side, when men rose up against us:

Then they had swallowed us up quick, when their wrath was kindled against us:

Then the waters had overwhelmed us, the stream had gone over our soul:

Then the proud waters had gone over our soul.

Blessed be the Lord, who hath not given us as a prey to their teeth.

Our soul is escaped as a bird out of the snare of the fowlers: the snare is broken, and we are escaped.

Our help is in the name of the Lord, who made heaven and earth.

Let this be your mantra for the day: "Our help is in the name of the Lord, who made heaven and earth."

ʻPsalm 125

They that trust in the Lord shall be as mount Zion, which
   cannot be removed, but abideth forever.
As the mountains are round about Jerusalem, so the Lord is
   round about his people from henceforth even forever.
For the rod of the wicked shall not rest upon the lot of the
   righteous; lest the righteous put forth their hands unto
   iniquity.
Do good, O Lord, unto those that be good, and to them that
   are upright in their hearts.
As for such as turn aside unto their crooked ways, the Lord shall
   lead them forth with the workers of iniquity: but peace
   shall be upon Israel.

What "crooked ways" must you turn away from?

Psalm 126

When the Lord turned again the captivity of Zion, we were like
    them that dream.
Then was our mouth filled with laughter, and our tongue with
    singing: then said they among the heathen, The Lord hath
    done great things for them.
The Lord hath done great things for us; whereof we are glad.
Turn again our captivity, O Lord, as the streams in the south.
They that sow in tears shall reap in joy.
He that goeth forth and weepeth, bearing precious seed, shall
    doubtless come again with rejoicing, bringing his sheaves
    with him.

This was recited by Israeli Prime Minister Menachem Begin during
the peace treaty between Egypt and Israel in 1979.
How does it speak to you today?

Psalm 127

Except the Lord build the house, they labor in vain that build it:
except the Lord keep the city, the watchman waketh but in
vain.

It is vain for you to rise up early, to sit up late, to eat the bread
of sorrows: for so he giveth his beloved sleep.

Lo, children are a heritage of the Lord: and the fruit of the
womb is his reward.

As arrows are in the hand of a mighty man; so are children of
the youth.

Happy is the man that hath his quiver full of them: they shall
not be ashamed, but they shall speak with the enemies in
the gate.

---

*Read Elizabeth Barrett Browning's poem "The Sleep," where
the end of each stanza is "He giveth his beloved sleep."
How does the poem compare with the psalm?*

Psalm 128

Blessed is every one that feareth the Lord; that walketh in his ways.
For thou shalt eat the labor of thine hands: happy shalt thou be,
   and it shall be well with thee.
Thy wife shall be as a fruitful vine by the sides of thine house:
   thy children like olive plants round about thy table.
Behold, that thus shall the man be blessed that feareth the Lord.
The Lord shall bless thee out of Zion: and thou shalt see the
   good of Jerusalem all the days of thy life.
Yea, thou shalt see thy children's children, and peace upon Israel.

What do you think about the imagery of the wife as "a fruitful vine"
and children "like olive plants"?

Psalm 129

Many a time have they afflicted me from my youth, may Israel
  now say:
Many a time have they afflicted me from my youth: yet they
  have not prevailed against me.
The plowers plowed upon my back: they made long their
  furrows.
The Lord is righteous: he hath cut asunder the cords of the
  wicked.
Let them all be confounded and turned back that hate Zion.
Let them be as the grass upon the housetops, which withereth
  afore it groweth up:
Wherewith the mower filleth not his hand; nor he that bindeth
  sheaves his bosom.
Neither do they which go by say, The blessing of the Lord be
  upon you: we bless you in the name of the Lord.

Who in your lifetime are "the plowers"
who "plowed upon [your] back"?

Psalm 130

Out of the depths have I cried unto thee, O Lord.
Lord, hear my voice: let thine ears be attentive to the voice of
    my supplications.
If thou, Lord, shouldest mark iniquities, O Lord, who shall stand?
But there is forgiveness with thee, that thou mayest be feared.
I wait for the Lord, my soul doth wait, and in his word do I hope.
My soul waiteth for the Lord more than they that watch for the
    morning: I say, more than they that watch for the morning.
Let Israel hope in the Lord: for with the Lord there is mercy,
    and with him is plenteous redemption.
And he shall redeem Israel from all his iniquities.

Ring a bell or sound a chime as you recite this psalm.

Psalm 131

Lord, my heart is not haughty, nor mine eyes lofty: neither do I
    exercise myself in great matters, or in things too high for me.
Surely I have behaved and quieted myself, as a child that is
    weaned of his mother: my soul is even as a weaned child.
Let Israel hope in the Lord from henceforth and forever.

This is one of three psalms with three verses.
Savor each verse, and let it fill your being.

ʹPsalm 132

Lord, remember David, and all his afflictions:

How he sware unto the Lord, and vowed unto the mighty God of Jacob;

Surely I will not come into the tabernacle of my house, nor go up into my bed;

I will not give sleep to mine eyes, or slumber to mine eyelids,

Until I find out a place for the Lord, a habitation for the mighty God of Jacob.

Lo, we heard of it at Ephratah: we found it in the fields of the wood.

We will go into his tabernacles: we will worship at his footstool.

Arise, O Lord, into thy rest; thou, and the ark of thy strength.

Let thy priests be clothed with righteousness; and let thy saints shout for joy.

For thy servant David's sake turn not away the face of thine anointed.

The Lord hath sworn in truth unto David; he will not turn from it; Of the fruit of thy body will I set upon thy throne.

If thy children will keep my covenant and my testimony that I shall teach them, their children shall also sit upon thy throne forevermore.

For the Lord hath chosen Zion; he hath desired it for his habitation.

This is my rest forever: here will I dwell; for I have desired it.

I will abundantly bless her provision: I will satisfy her poor with bread.

I will also clothe her priests with salvation: and her saints shall shout aloud for joy.

There will I make the horn of David to bud: I have ordained a lamp for mine anointed.

His enemies will I clothe with shame: but upon himself shall his crown flourish.

Where is your Zion? Where do you experience the presence of God?

_____

_____

_____

_____

Psalm 133

Behold, how good and how pleasant it is for brethren to dwell
together in unity!

It is like the precious ointment upon the head, that ran down
upon the beard, even Aaron's beard: that went down to the
skirts of his garments;

As the dew of Hermon, and as the dew that descended upon
the mountains of Zion: for there the Lord commanded the
blessing, even life forevermore.

_Would you characterize your relationships with others
as "dwelling in unity"?_

Psalm 134

Behold, bless ye the Lord, all ye servants of the Lord, which by
night stand in the house of the Lord.
Lift up your hands in the sanctuary, and bless the Lord.
The Lord that made heaven and earth bless thee out of Zion.

Pray this psalm in the night and note what feelings settle in you.

Psalm 135

Praise ye the Lord. Praise ye the name of the Lord; praise him,
O ye servants of the Lord.

Ye that stand in the house of the Lord, in the courts of the
house of our God,

Praise the Lord; for the Lord is good: sing praises unto his
name; for it is pleasant.

For the Lord hath chosen Jacob unto himself, and Israel for his
peculiar treasure.

For I know that the Lord is great, and that our Lord is above all
gods.

Whatsoever the Lord pleased, that did he in heaven, and in
earth, in the seas, and all deep places.

He causeth the vapors to ascend from the ends of the earth; he
maketh lightnings for the rain; he bringeth the wind out of
his treasuries.

Who smote the firstborn of Egypt, both of man and beast.

Who sent tokens and wonders into the midst of thee, O Egypt,
upon Pharaoh, and upon all his servants.

Who smote great nations, and slew mighty kings;

Sihon king of the Amorites, and Og king of Bashan, and all the
kingdoms of Canaan:

And gave their land for a heritage, a heritage unto Israel his
people.

Thy name, O Lord, endureth forever; and thy memorial,
O Lord, throughout all generations.

For the Lord will judge his people, and he will repent himself
concerning his servants.

The idols of the heathen are silver and gold, the work of men's
hands.

They have mouths, but they speak not; eyes have they, but they
see not;

They have ears, but they hear not; neither is there any breath in their mouths.

They that make them are like unto them: so is every one that trusteth in them.

Bless the Lord, O house of Israel: bless the Lord, O house of Aaron:

Bless the Lord, O house of Levi: ye that fear the Lord, bless the Lord.

Blessed be the Lord out of Zion, which dwelleth at Jerusalem. Praise ye the Lord.

As with this psalm, which begins and ends with "Praise ye the Lord," start and end your day with this phrase and note how it makes you feel.

Psalm 136

O give thanks unto the Lord, for he is good: for his mercy endureth forever.

O give thanks unto the God of gods: for his mercy endureth forever.

O give thanks to the Lord of lords: for his mercy endureth forever.

To him who alone doeth great wonders: for his mercy endureth forever.

To him that by wisdom made the heavens: for his mercy endureth forever.

To him that stretched out the earth above the waters: for his mercy endureth forever.

To him that made great lights: for his mercy endureth forever:

The sun to rule by day: for his mercy endureth forever:

The moon and stars to rule by night: for his mercy endureth forever.

To him that smote Egypt in their firstborn: for his mercy endureth forever:

And brought out Israel from among them: for his mercy endureth forever:

With a strong hand, and with a stretched out arm: for his mercy endureth forever.

To him which divided the Red sea into parts: for his mercy endureth forever:

And made Israel to pass through the midst of it: for his mercy endureth forever:

But overthrew Pharaoh and his host in the Red sea: for his mercy endureth forever.

To him which led his people through the wilderness: for his mercy endureth forever.

To him which smote great kings: for his mercy endureth forever:

And slew famous kings: for his mercy endureth forever:
Sihon king of the Amorites: for his mercy endureth forever:
And Og the king of Bashan: for his mercy endureth forever:
And gave their land for a heritage: for his mercy endureth
    forever:
Even a heritage unto Israel his servant: for his mercy endureth
    forever.
Who remembered us in our low estate: for his mercy endureth
    forever:
And hath redeemed us from our enemies: for his mercy
    endureth forever.
Who giveth food to all flesh: for his mercy endureth forever.
O give thanks unto the God of heaven: for his mercy endureth
    forever.

---

*If you were to compose a psalm that told a story about why
God's mercy endures forever, what would it be about?*

Psalm 137

By the rivers of Babylon, there we sat down, yea, we wept,
  when we remembered Zion.
We hanged our harps upon the willows in the midst thereof.
For there they that carried us away captive required of us a
  song; and they that wasted us required of us mirth, saying,
  Sing us one of the songs of Zion.
How shall we sing the Lord's song in a strange land?
If I forget thee, O Jerusalem, let my right hand forget her cunning.
If I do not remember thee, let my tongue cleave to the roof of
  my mouth; if I prefer not Jerusalem above my chief joy.
Remember, O Lord, the children of Edom in the day of Jerusalem;
  who said, Rase it, rase it, even to the foundation thereof.
O daughter of Babylon, who art to be destroyed; happy shall he
  be, that rewardeth thee as thou hast served us.
Happy shall he be, that taketh and dasheth thy little ones
  against the stones.

Give a listen to "Rivers of Babylon" by the Melodians,
"On the Willows" from Godspell, and "By the Rivers Dark"
by Leonard Cohen, all based on this psalm.

Psalm 138

I will praise thee with my whole heart: before the gods will I
     sing praise unto thee.
I will worship toward thy holy temple, and praise thy name
     for thy loving-kindness and for thy truth: for thou hast
     magnified thy word above all thy name.
In the day when I cried thou answeredst me, and strengthenedst
     me with strength in my soul.
All the kings of the earth shall praise thee, O Lord, when they
     hear the words of thy mouth.
Yea, they shall sing in the ways of the Lord: for great is the
     glory of the Lord.
Though the Lord be high, yet hath he respect unto the lowly:
     but the proud he knoweth afar off.
Though I walk in the midst of trouble, thou wilt revive me: thou
     shalt stretch forth thine hand against the wrath of mine
     enemies, and thy right hand shall save me.
The Lord will perfect that which concerneth me: thy mercy,
     O Lord, endureth forever: forsake not the works of thine
     own hands.

What would your song of thanksgiving say?

ʻPsalm 139

O Lord, thou hast searched me, and known me.

Thou knowest my downsitting and mine uprising; thou
understandest my thought afar off.

Thou compassest my path and my lying down, and art
acquainted with all my ways.

For there is not a word in my tongue, but, lo, O Lord, thou
knowest it altogether.

Thou hast beset me behind and before, and laid thine hand
upon me.

Such knowledge is too wonderful for me; it is high, I cannot
attain unto it.

Whither shall I go from thy Spirit? or whither shall I flee from
thy presence?

If I ascend up into heaven, thou art there: if I make my bed in
hell, behold, thou art there.

If I take the wings of the morning, and dwell in the uttermost
parts of the sea;

Even there shall thy hand lead me, and thy right hand shall
hold me.

If I say, Surely the darkness shall cover me; even the night shall
be light about me.

Yea, the darkness hideth not from thee; but the night shineth as
the day: the darkness and the light are both alike to thee.

For thou hast possessed my reins: thou hast covered me in my
mother's womb.

I will praise thee; for I am fearfully and wonderfully made:
marvelous are thy works; and that my soul knoweth right
well.

My substance was not hid from thee when I was made in secret,
and curiously wrought in the lowest parts of the earth.

Thine eyes did see my substance, yet being unperfect; and
　　in thy book all my members were written, which in
　　continuance were fashioned, when as yet there was none of
　　them.
How precious also are thy thoughts unto me, O God! how great
　　is the sum of them!
If I should count them, they are more in number than the sand:
　　when I awake, I am still with thee.
Surely thou wilt slay the wicked, O God: depart from me
　　therefore, ye bloody men.
For they speak against thee wickedly, and thine enemies take
　　thy name in vain.
Do not I hate them, O Lord, that hate thee? and am not I
　　grieved with those that rise up against thee?
I hate them with perfect hatred: I count them mine enemies.
Search me, O God, and know my heart: try me, and know my
　　thoughts:
And see if there be any wicked way in me, and lead me in the
　　way everlasting.

---

*How does it make you feel that God fully knows
and understands you?*

Psalm 140

Deliver me, O Lord, from the evil man: preserve me from the
violent man;

Which imagine mischiefs in their heart; continually are they
gathered together for war.

They have sharpened their tongues like a serpent; adders'
poison is under their lips. Selah.

Keep me, O Lord, from the hands of the wicked; preserve me from
the violent man; who have purposed to overthrow my goings.

The proud have hid a snare for me, and cords; they have spread
a net by the wayside; they have set gins for me. Selah.

I said unto the Lord, Thou art my God: hear the voice of my
supplications, O Lord.

O God the Lord, the strength of my salvation, thou hast
covered my head in the day of battle.

Grant not, O Lord, the desires of the wicked: further not his
wicked device; lest they exalt themselves. Selah.

As for the head of those that compass me about, let the mischief
of their own lips cover them.

Let burning coals fall upon them: let them be cast into the fire;
into deep pits, that they rise not up again.

Let not an evil speaker be established in the earth: evil shall
hunt the violent man to overthrow him.

I know that the Lord will maintain the cause of the afflicted, and
the right of the poor.

Surely the righteous shall give thanks unto thy name: the
upright shall dwell in thy presence.

---

*Selah means "to stop and listen." Do this after each section
of this psalm to let the passage sink in.*

'Psalm 141

Lord, I cry unto thee: make haste unto me; give ear unto my
voice, when I cry unto thee.

Let my prayer be set forth before thee as incense; and the lifting
up of my hands as the evening sacrifice.

Set a watch, O Lord, before my mouth; keep the door of my lips.

Incline not my heart to any evil thing, to practise wicked works with
men that work iniquity: and let me not eat of their dainties.

Let the righteous smite me; it shall be a kindness: and let him
reprove me; it shall be an excellent oil, which shall not break
my head: for yet my prayer also shall be in their calamities.

When their judges are overthrown in stony places, they shall
hear my words; for they are sweet.

Our bones are scattered at the grave's mouth, as when one
cutteth and cleaveth wood upon the earth.

But mine eyes are unto thee, O God the Lord: in thee is my
trust; leave not my soul destitute.

Keep me from the snares which they have laid for me, and the
gins of the workers of iniquity.

Let the wicked fall into their own nets, whilst that I withal escape.

What specific evil do you want to keep from saying and feeling,
for which you cry out for help?

'Psalm 142

I cried unto the Lord with my voice; with my voice unto the
   Lord did I make my supplication.
I poured out my complaint before him; I showed before him my
   trouble.
When my spirit was overwhelmed within me, then thou
   knewest my path. In the way wherein I walked have they
   privily laid a snare for me.
I looked on my right hand, and beheld, but there was no man
   that would know me: refuge failed me; no man cared for my
   soul.
I cried unto thee, O Lord: I said, Thou art my refuge and my
   portion in the land of the living.
Attend unto my cry; for I am brought very low: deliver me from
   my persecutors; for they are stronger than I.
Bring my soul out of prison, that I may praise thy name: the
   righteous shall compass me about; for thou shalt deal
   bountifully with me.

*Saint Francis of Assisi is said to have recited this psalm
on his deathbed. Does it capture what you
would want to pray if you were on yours?*

Psalm 143

Hear my prayer, O Lord, give ear to my supplications: in thy faithfulness answer me, and in thy righteousness.

And enter not into judgment with thy servant: for in thy sight shall no man living be justified.

For the enemy hath persecuted my soul; he hath smitten my life down to the ground; he hath made me to dwell in darkness, as those that have been long dead.

Therefore is my spirit overwhelmed within me; my heart within me is desolate.

I remember the days of old; I meditate on all thy works; I muse on the work of thy hands.

I stretch forth my hands unto thee: my soul thirsteth after thee, as a thirsty land. Selah.

Hear me speedily, O Lord; my spirit faileth: hide not thy face from me, lest I be like unto them that go down into the pit.

Cause me to hear thy loving-kindness in the morning; for in thee do I trust: cause me to know the way wherein I should walk; for I lift up my soul unto thee.

Deliver me, O Lord, from mine enemies: I flee unto thee to hide me.

Teach me to do thy will; for thou art my God: thy Spirit is good; lead me into the land of uprightness.

Quicken me, O Lord, for thy name's sake: for thy righteousness' sake bring my soul out of trouble.

And of thy mercy cut off mine enemies, and destroy all them that afflict my soul: for I am thy servant.

Use this as your mandate for the day: "Cause me to hear thy loving-kindness in the morning . . . cause me to know the way wherein I should walk."

Psalm 144

Blessed be the Lord my strength, which teacheth my hands to
    war, and my fingers to fight:

My goodness, and my fortress; my high tower, and my
    deliverer; my shield, and he in whom I trust; who subdueth
    my people under me.

Lord, what is man, that thou takest knowledge of him! or the
    son of man, that thou makest account of him!

Man is like to vanity: his days are as a shadow that passeth
    away.

Bow thy heavens, O Lord, and come down: touch the
    mountains, and they shall smoke.

Cast forth lightning, and scatter them: shoot out thine arrows,
    and destroy them.

Send thine hand from above; rid me, and deliver me out of great
    waters, from the hand of strange children;

Whose mouth speaketh vanity, and their right hand is a right
    hand of falsehood.

I will sing a new song unto thee, O God: upon a psaltery and an
    instrument of ten strings will I sing praises unto thee.

It is he that giveth salvation unto kings: who delivereth David
    his servant from the hurtful sword.

Rid me, and deliver me from the hand of strange children,
    whose mouth speaketh vanity, and their right hand is a
    right hand of falsehood:

That our sons may be as plants grown up in their youth; that
    our daughters may be as corner stones, polished after the
    similitude of a palace:

That our garners may be full, affording all manner of store; that
    our sheep may bring forth thousands and ten thousands in
    our streets:

That our oxen may be strong to labor; that there be no breaking in, nor going out; that there be no complaining in our streets. Happy is that people, that is in such a case: yea, happy is that people, whose God is the Lord.

The psalmist says God is "My goodness, and my fortress; my high tower, and my deliverer; my shield." What is God to you?

Psalm 145

I will extol thee, my God, O King; and I will bless thy name
forever and ever.

Every day will I bless thee; and I will praise thy name forever
and ever.

Great is the Lord, and greatly to be praised; and his greatness is
unsearchable.

One generation shall praise thy works to another, and shall
declare thy mighty acts.

I will speak of the glorious honor of thy majesty, and of thy
wondrous works.

And men shall speak of the might of thy terrible acts: and I will
declare thy greatness.

They shall abundantly utter the memory of thy great goodness,
and shall sing of thy righteousness.

The Lord is gracious, and full of compassion; slow to anger, and
of great mercy.

The Lord is good to all: and his tender mercies are over all his
works.

All thy works shall praise thee, O Lord; and thy saints shall
bless thee.

They shall speak of the glory of thy kingdom, and talk of thy
power;

To make known to the sons of men his mighty acts, and the
glorious majesty of his kingdom.

Thy kingdom is an everlasting kingdom, and thy dominion
endureth throughout all generations.

The Lord upholdeth all that fall, and raiseth up all those that be
bowed down.

The eyes of all wait upon thee; and thou givest them their meat
in due season.

Thou openest thine hand, and satisfiest the desire of every
living thing.

The Lord is righteous in all his ways, and holy in all his works.

The Lord is nigh unto all them that call upon him, to all that call upon him in truth.

He will fulfil the desire of them that fear him: he also will hear their cry, and will save them.

The Lord preserveth all them that love him: but all the wicked will he destroy.

My mouth shall speak the praise of the Lord: and let all flesh bless his holy name forever and ever.

Contemplate God's greatness in your life.

Psalm 146

Praise ye the Lord. Praise the Lord, O my soul.

While I live will I praise the Lord: I will sing praises unto my
God while I have any being.

Put not your trust in princes, nor in the son of man, in whom
there is no help.

His breath goeth forth, he returneth to his earth; in that very
day his thoughts perish.

Happy is he that hath the God of Jacob for his help, whose
hope is in the Lord his God:

Which made heaven, and earth, the sea, and all that therein is:
which keepeth truth forever:

Which executeth judgment for the oppressed: which giveth
food to the hungry. The Lord looseth the prisoners:

The Lord openeth the eyes of the blind: the Lord raiseth them
that are bowed down: the Lord loveth the righteous:

The Lord preserveth the strangers; he relieveth the fatherless
and widow: but the way of the wicked he turneth upside
down.

The Lord shall reign forever, even thy God, O Zion, unto all
generations. Praise ye the Lord.

---

*It is said that God frees prisoners, makes the blind see, lifts up
those who are bowed down, loves the righteous, watches over the
foreigner, sustains the fatherless and the widow, and frustrates the
wicked. How do you see God working in the world? In your life?*

Psalm 147

Praise ye the Lord: for it is good to sing praises unto our God;
for it is pleasant; and praise is comely.

The Lord doth build up Jerusalem: he gathereth together the
outcasts of Israel.

He healeth the broken in heart, and bindeth up their wounds.

He telleth the number of the stars; he calleth them all by their
names.

Great is our Lord, and of great power: his understanding is
infinite.

The Lord lifteth up the meek: he casteth the wicked down to
the ground.

Sing unto the Lord with thanksgiving; sing praise upon the harp
unto our God:

Who covereth the heaven with clouds, who prepareth rain for
the earth, who maketh grass to grow upon the mountains.

He giveth to the beast his food, and to the young ravens which
cry.

He delighteth not in the strength of the horse: he taketh not
pleasure in the legs of a man.

The Lord taketh pleasure in them that fear him, in those that
hope in his mercy.

Praise the Lord, O Jerusalem; praise thy God, O Zion.

For he hath strengthened the bars of thy gates; he hath blessed
thy children within thee.

He maketh peace in thy borders, and filleth thee with the finest
of the wheat.

He sendeth forth his commandment upon earth: his word
runneth very swiftly.

He giveth snow like wool: he scattereth the hoar frost like
ashes.

He casteth forth his ice like morsels: who can stand before his
cold?

He sendeth out his word, and melteth them: he causeth his
    wind to blow, and the waters flow.
He showeth his word unto Jacob, his statutes and his judgments
    unto Israel.
He hath not dealt so with any nation: and as for his judgments,
    they have not known them. Praise ye the Lord.

This is a psalm of praise. Create your own.

Psalm 148

Praise ye the Lord. Praise ye the Lord from the heavens: praise
    him in the heights.
Praise ye him, all his angels: praise ye him, all his hosts.
Praise ye him, sun and moon: praise him, all ye stars of light.
Praise him, ye heavens of heavens, and ye waters that be above
    the heavens.
Let them praise the name of the Lord: for he commanded, and
    they were created.
He hath also stablished them forever and ever: he hath made a
    decree which shall not pass.
Praise the Lord from the earth, ye dragons, and all deeps:
Fire, and hail; snow, and vapor; stormy wind fulfilling his word:
Mountains, and all hills; fruitful trees, and all cedars:
Beasts, and all cattle; creeping things, and flying fowl:
Kings of the earth, and all people; princes, and all judges of the
    earth:
Both young men, and maidens; old men, and children:
Let them praise the name of the Lord: for his name alone is
    excellent; his glory is above the earth and heaven.
He also exalteth the horn of his people, the praise of all his
    saints; even of the children of Israel, a people near unto
    him. Praise ye the Lord.

*This is the first of three Laudate psalms, which are traditionally
sung together as a morning prayer. Go ahead and try this.*

Psalm 149

Praise ye the Lord. Sing unto the Lord a new song, and his
    praise in the congregation of saints.
Let Israel rejoice in him that made him: let the children of Zion
    be joyful in their King.
Let them praise his name in the dance: let them sing praises
    unto him with the timbrel and harp.
For the Lord taketh pleasure in his people: he will beautify the
    meek with salvation.
Let the saints be joyful in glory: let them sing aloud upon their
    beds.
Let the high praises of God be in their mouth, and a two-edged
    sword in their hand;
To execute vengeance upon the heathen, and punishments upon
    the people;
To bind their kings with chains, and their nobles with fetters of
    iron;
To execute upon them the judgment written: this honor have all
    his saints. Praise ye the Lord.

This is the second of three Laudate psalms.
Make up your own song of rejoicing.

Psalm 150

Praise ye the Lord. Praise God in his sanctuary: praise him in the firmament of his power.

Praise him for his mighty acts: praise him according to his excellent greatness.

Praise him with the sound of the trumpet: praise him with the psaltery and harp.

Praise him with the timbrel and dance: praise him with stringed instruments and organs.

Praise him upon the loud cymbals: praise him upon the high sounding cymbals.

Let every thing that hath breath praise the Lord. Praise ye the Lord.

This is the third of three Laudate psalms.
Play music and dance in celebration of life!